George Friedman

THE STORM BEFORE THE CALM

George Friedman is the founder and chairman of Geopolitical Futures, which specializes in geopolitical forecasting. Prior to this, Friedman was chairman of the global intelligence company Stratfor, which he founded in 1996. Friedman is the author of six books, including the *New York Times* bestsellers *The Next Decade* and *The Next 100 Years*. He lives in Austin, Texas.

www.geopoliticalfutures.com

THE STORM
BEFORE
THE CALM

Climat change ← an incomplete model
              only negative outcomes.

THE STORM
BEFORE
THE CALM

AMERICA'S DISCORD, THE CRISIS OF THE
2020S, AND THE TRIUMPH BEYOND

George Friedman

ANCHOR BOOKS
A Division of Penguin Random House LLC
New York

FIRST ANCHOR BOOKS EDITION, JANUARY 2021

Copyright © 2020 by George Friedman
Preface copyright © 2021 by George Friedman

The Library of Congress has cataloged the Doubleday edition as follows:
Names: Friedman, George, author.
Title: The storm before the calm : America's discord, the crisis of the 2020s,
and the triumph beyond / George Friedman.
Description: First edition. | New York : Doubleday, 2020.
Identifiers: LCCN 2019032726 (print) | LCCN 2019032727 (ebook)
Subjects: LCSH: Twenty-first century—Forecasts. | United States—Politics and
government—21st century—Forecasting. | United States—Foreign relations—21st
century—Forecasting. | United States—Economic conditions—21st century—
Forecasting. | United States—Civilization—21st century—Forecasting.
Classification: LCC E893 .F75 2020 (print) | LCC E893 (ebook) | DDC
909.83—dc23
LC record available at https://lccn.loc.gov/2019032726

Anchor Books Trade Paperback ISBN: 978-1-101-91178-5
eBook ISBN: 978-0-385-54050-6

Illustrations created by Stacy Haren from Geopolitical Futures.
Maps and charts created by Geopolitical Futures.
Author photograph © Meredith Friedman
Book design by Michael Collica

www.anchorbooks.com

Printed in the United States of America
10   9   8   7   6   5   4

Dedicated to the future of America, my grandchildren:
Ethan, Austin, Mira, Asher, Ari, Kathryn, Nicholas, and Douglass

It was the best of times, it was the worst of times, it was the age of wisdom, it was the age of foolishness, it was the epoch of belief, it was the epoch of incredulity, it was the season of light, it was the season of darkness, it was the spring of hope, it was the winter of despair. We had everything before us, we had nothing before us. We were all going direct to Heaven, we were all going direct the other way—in short, the period was so far like the present period, that some of its noisiest authorities insisted on its being received for good or evil, in the superlative degree of comparison only.

—Charles Dickens

Contents

CONTENTS

List of Illustrations

Preface

I wrote this book in anticipation of the 2020s. Using history as a guide, I predicted an intensely difficult period of social and economic tension, culminating in a shift in how America works, beginning around 2030 and working its way through society in the following decade. I noted that every fifty years or so, the nation goes through a cycle of wrenching socioeconomic crisis, the last one starting in the late 1960s and ending in the 1980s.

I also noted a second cycle—the eighty-year institutional cycle, starting with the American Revolution, reemerging in the Civil War, and shifting again in World War II. In 2025, it will be eighty years since the end of World War II. In 2030, it will have been fifty years since Ronald Reagan came to power. I expected the 2020s to be a particularly tense period since these two cycles, the socioeconomic and the institutional, have never bottomed out during the same decade, as they are doing now. There have been terrible moments in American history: the institutional shift ushered in by the Civil War, the socioeconomic shift driven by the Great Depression, and so on. I don't expect civil war and doubt there will be a depression, but still, we are in for a rough period.

It has certainly been rough so far, largely because of something I did not anticipate and could not have predicted: a virus that has killed, as of this writing, 1,150,961 people globally and 224,221 in the United States and counting. There are various vaccines in the works, but until there is a trusted and effective vaccine on the market, our only defense is to fundamentally change how we live.

Oddly enough, the pandemic has not undermined my forecast. It has accelerated it. I predicted that the 2020s would open with a moderate but global recession, leading to great social tension. COVID-19 delivered that on steroids. Certainly the greatest danger of the pandemic is massive loss of life, but another insidious danger is that it might lead to a depression. The Great Depression claimed the lives of many through hunger, cold, and disease. We have not had a depression in the United States for nearly a century, so there's a lot we don't understand.

A recession is a normal part of a business cycle, a financial event that culls weak businesses. A depression is very different. It destroys parts of the economy, bankrupting businesses and costing jobs that will not exist again. It is a long-term disease. So far, the United States has seen the devastation of brick-and-mortar retail, and COVID-19 has caused the airlines to contract. But retail was already being destroyed by online sales, and airlines still own airplanes and there are still airports. They can bounce back. So we are not yet in a depression, and that means for now my forecast is intact. We are in a worse recession than I expected, but it is not a depression.

However, the pandemic has drawn attention to the institutional crisis. The problem I lay out in this book is the loss of confidence in experts among the public. The medical profession has focused on ways to limit infection. Outside their area of expertise, however, is the economic consequence of the medical solution. The solution is social distancing, which in turn removes large numbers of people from the workforce and creates its own economic problem for those who are unable to work.

Also less considered by the medical experts or the economists are the social consequences. Children do far more in school than study.

They enter a world in which their wishes do not take precedence, a world where they must learn to collaborate with other children. The children are relatively safe from the virus and not directly touched by the economic damage, but if children are isolated from other children for a year or two at the age of five, how does this affect their social development?

The point is that the rule of the expert, or the technocrat, which dominated the last institutional cycle, creates decisions that are frequently indifferent to consequences outside the expert's field. The expert is a fox, as Aesop's fable said, who knows one thing very well. He is not a hedgehog who knows many things, and the ability of the political structure to make decisions based on widely disparate experts, all claiming priority, leads to the chaos we have seen and points to the end of this posture. Expertise is essential, but a means of integrating expertise with common sense as the prime driver will be the challenge of the next institutional cycle.

COVID-19 surprised me. The rest did not, particularly the rise of social instability driven by the opposition to racism. As I and others have said, slavery was the original sin of America, and its consequences continue to haunt us, persisting even with the best intentions and generating tremendous periodic tension. It is not surprising that the first non-COVID-19 event that opened the 2020s was an intense rising against racism. The last socioeconomic cycle began with the murder of Martin Luther King, Jr., and rioting in many cities, including Detroit, where the 82nd Airborne was deployed. Many radical black organizations emerged. The police were called pigs, and the Black movement was linked to the predominantly white anti-war movement. The intensity was overwhelming. Richard Nixon was seen as a murderer and racist.

Race, one way or another, was the first signal of a cyclical shift, as it has been in previous cycles. In the 1920s, the Ku Klux Klan was a significant power going far beyond the South. The previous cycle, beginning in the 1870s, came right after the Civil War, which was very much about slavery. Each of the last three cycles opened with deep racial tension. Now the fourth has begun this way as well.

In the midst of all this, we face a presidential election. As I write this, I don't know who will win. I can say that in terms of changing the shape of our history, the election will matter little. After Nixon was forced from office, Ford and Carter could not change the reality. Warren G. Harding was likely a criminal, but Calvin Coolidge and Herbert Hoover were not. Yet none of them could change the direction of things. The power of the system can be overwhelming, and while we wait for our presidents to transform the world for us, reality limits them in what they can do.

Trump, like Nixon, was able to involve himself in some mayhem and to appear responsible for all that was bad to his enemies and all that was good to his friends. But in the end, the basic structure of American society was unchanged. Trump will end his presidency in one or two terms, and then a Ford or Coolidge will take his place, with the hope that the great national nightmare is over, to quote Gerald Ford. It wasn't, but everyone was exhausted. It didn't end until 1980 when Reagan became president and reality forced him to do what was necessary at that time. Necessity, not goodwill or sweeping visions, define what will happen next in the United States, and even presidents serve that necessity. The American system, as I describe in the coming pages, is built on a weak presidency, coupled with a bully pulpit that allows presidents to appear more important than they are. History is patient, and that patience will be needed until at least 2028, when a failing system will force itself to be replaced.

October 27, 2020

THE STORM
BEFORE
THE CALM

Introduction

The United States is living through a difficult time. Americans are focused on Donald Trump's presidency. His enemies believe him to be corrupt and incompetent. His supporters regard him as the victim of an entrenched elite wanting to destroy him. Much of the tension focuses on Trump, as if he alone were the problem or the solution.

There is nothing new about this. The kind of mutual rage and division we see in America today is trivial compared with other times in U.S. history—the Civil War, in which 650,000 died, or the 1960s, when the Eighty-Second Airborne was deployed to fight snipers in Detroit. Abraham Lincoln was called illiterate and an ape. Richard Nixon was called a criminal, which he turned out to be, even though he blamed it all on the media. Some presidents like Lincoln, Nixon, and Trump are reviled by some and loved by others, but the reality is they are not powerful enough to be causing the problems—nor in control of the underlying currents they are riding.

Americans place a great deal of emphasis on the president, going back to Washington, Jackson, or Lincoln. This is ironic, because the American president has little power compared with European prime ministers. The founders set this up intentionally, and this arrangement has stood the test of time. A president faces two parliaments, countless federal judges, and fifty sovereign states. He can rarely achieve anything, but he focuses the mind of the nation. So, when the nation goes through one of its periodic and predictable crises, rather than understanding the impersonal forces driving events, Americans blame or praise the president.

This is a book that focuses on the underlying process in American history, explaining this moment we are in within the context of our broader history and putting the current passions into context. It will also explain the very real coming crisis of the 2020s–2030s and ultimately show how the United States will deal with the pain and confusion and emerge on the other side stronger and more dynamic.

At the moment, a series of deep structural changes are taking place in the United States, and these changes are creating profound stresses. The federal government is undergoing a periodic shift in which its operations and traditional relationships to society are changing. That shift is driven by increasing failure in the system. Simultaneously, the economic system is undergoing a fundamental shift driven partly by an excess of money and limited opportunity for investment. This in turn results in a massive decline in productivity growth due to a falloff in innovation. Between these two stresses, and the pressure that emerged from the United States trying to find its balance in the global system, the glue that was holding American society together has weakened and will continue to decline throughout the 2020s. And regardless of who is president, fear and loathing will stalk the land for another decade.

This is not the first time this has happened, by any means.

If we step back and take the long view, there are two major cycles in American history, and by understanding these cycles, we can understand the situation in the United States today. One is the "institutional cycle," which has transpired approximately every eighty years. The first institutional cycle began with the end of the Revolutionary War and the drafting of the Constitution in the mid-1780s and ended in 1865 with the Civil War. The second institutional cycle ended eighty years later with the end of World War II. The strains of the next transition are becoming obvious now and will take place around 2025.

The second major cycle is the "socioeconomic," which has occurred approximately every fifty years. The last shift happened around 1980, when the economic and social dysfunction that began in the late 1960s culminated with a fundamental shift in how the economic and social systems functioned. As I will explain in more detail in later chapters, the previous socioeconomic cycle changed in the early 1930s after the Great Depression started, and, before that, in the 1880s as the country refocused after the Civil War. We are now facing another period of social and economic instability that will conclude in the late 2020s.

In looking at these two major cycles, we see something we have not seen before. The current institutional cycle will conclude in a crisis around the mid-2020s, and the socioeconomic cycle will end in a crisis within a few years of that. This is the first time in American history that the two cycles will culminate so close together, practically overlapping. That obviously means that the 2020s will be one of the more difficult periods in American history, particularly when we consider the new and complex role the United States plays in the world—something that was not a factor during nearly all earlier cycles. The Trump administration, therefore, is only the precursor of this period and of what's to come. This is not about Donald Trump, positive or negative. He can be perceived as either bold and brash or incompetent and uncouth, but when we look beyond the details, he—and we—are simply passengers on the American roller coaster.

It should be remembered that each of these American socioeconomic cycles ended in a period of confidence and prosperity. The Civil War was followed by a tremendous growth period where thirty-five years later the United States was producing half of the manufactured goods of the world; World War II was followed by an unprecedented growth of a mass professional class; and the Cold

3

War was followed by the tech boom that changed the world. I am not predicting doom. I am predicting an intensely difficult period of time between now and when the next phase of American history begins in the early 2030s—and the period of confidence and prosperity that will follow it.

It's important to note that unlike what sometimes happens in other nations, these cycles don't break the United States. Rather they drive it forward. The cycles represent the engine driving the United States. Each period begins with a problem generated by the previous cycle, creates a new model from which to draw on American strength, and culminates in that solution playing out its hand and becoming the new problem that has to be solved.

It is the orderliness and rapidity of these cycles that are striking. Where in other countries the cycles are much more unpredictable in timing and intensity, the American cycles have been highly predictable and frequent. This has to do with the velocity and agility with which America developed. That in turn was the result of the structure of the United States: its regime, its people, and its land. All of these created a platform not only for rapid growth but for managing the growth. A nation's growth can't be linear. Old systems that have outworn their utility have to be destroyed, and new systems have to be created. The nature of the United States has always facilitated this, and as I will examine in the coming chapters, it will continue to do so.

The most important fact to bear in mind is that the United States was an invented nation; it didn't evolve naturally from a finite group of people over thousands of years in one indigenous region, as did, for example, China or Russia. More than that, the United States was an intentionally and rapidly invented nation. The American regime was first conceived in the Declaration of Independence and institutionalized in the Constitution. The American people were constructed from many countries and many languages, with varied reasons for coming to America—most freely, and some by force.

The people of the United States invented themselves from a blank slate. And in important ways the American land invented itself. It provided Americans with possibilities that were unimaginable to most and could be used in ways no one anticipated.

The regime, the people, and the land combine to give the nation agility most other nations lack. The regime was built to be flexible and to leave the people free to evolve as quickly as they could take advantage of the land. It allows the United States to develop with an extraordinary speed. And because all things must exhaust themselves at some point, it also leads to frequent crises that seem about to break the nation. But instead, America actually refuels itself from the crises, re-forming itself with a remarkable agility.

I have divided this book into three parts. Part 1 seeks to explain the American character, American values, and the history that led to the formation of the "American people." It also shows why the United States is so resilient and why it can survive extreme periods. Part 2 describes the two major cycles in detail and the realities that govern American history, especially what has led to the crisis the United States is currently experiencing. Part 3 is a forecast for the future, describing the crisis that will happen when the massive forces of these two cycles converge in the decade 2020 to 2030—something that has not happened before—and then looks at what will follow and the future of America when the storm has passed.

This book is the story of how the United States works beneath the surface. To understand that, we must begin with grasping the texture of the American regime, people, and land. The true story of the United States is how it systematically changes its shape in order to grow. And that means we must understand the shape of the United States from its founding, and then move on to how the cycles work, and what they portend for the future.

PART ONE

THE INVENTION OF AMERICA

1

The American Regime and
a Restless Nation

On the last day of the Constitutional Convention, right after adoption, a woman waiting outside the old Pennsylvania State House asked Benjamin Franklin whether the nation would be a monarchy or a republic. His answer was "A Republic, if you can keep it." The Constitutional Convention invented the American government. It was an invention in two ways. First, it created a government where none had existed. Second, it created a machine, the machinery of government, which had sprung from the minds of the founders. Unlike other governments, it had no past. This government came into existence through design, architecture, and engineering.

The machine was built on two principles. First, the founders feared government, because governments tended to accumulate power and become tyrannies. Second, they did not trust the people, because the people—in pursuing their private interests—might divert the government from the common good. Government was necessary, and so of course were citizens, but both had to be restrained in such a way that the machinery of government limited their ability to accumulate power. The founders had created such a machine.

The founders were trying to invent a machine that restrained itself, thereby creating a vast terrain in American life that was free from government or politics. They sought to create a sphere of private life in which citizens would pursue the happiness that had been promised in the Declaration of Independence. The private sphere would be the sphere of commerce, industry, religion, and the endless pleasures that were the domain of private life. The most important thing about the machine they invented was the degree to which it was restrained from intruding on the things they held most important, the things that were not political.

It is one thing to invent a machine and another to make it run without extensive maintenance. The solution for this invention was to make it inefficient. The balance of powers that were created achieved three important things: first, it made the passage of laws enormously difficult; second, the president would be incapable of becoming a tyrant; and third, Congress would be limited by the courts in what it could achieve. The founders' remarkably inefficient system of government did what it was designed to do; it did little, and the little that it did, it did poorly. The government had to protect the nation and maintain a degree of internal trade. But it was private life that would create a cycle of creativity that would allow society, economy, and institutions to evolve at remarkable speed yet not end up tearing the country apart, save for some near misses. This is why Benjamin Franklin left the Pennsylvania State House in Philadelphia both confident and cautious. He knew that the regime was designed to balance powerful and dangerous forces, and he knew that it was a new and untried form of government.

This was not simply a matter of the legal phrases contained in the Constitution. It was even more a matter of creating and enshrining moral principles, some only implicit and others clearly stated. Limits on society, both public and private, can be imposed not by political fiat or documents but by rendering the extraordinary moral vision as merely the common sense of the nation. The moral principles were complex and sometimes at odds with each other, but they had a common core: each American ought to be free to succeed or fail in the things he wished to undertake.

This was the meaning of the idea of the right to pursue happiness. The state would not hinder anyone. A person's fate would be determined only by his character and talents. The founders did more than separate the state and private life. They created an ongoing tension between them. Visit a meeting of any local public school board, where the realities of the government meet the needs of the people. The desire not to have increased taxes—but to deliver increased services—confronts a government that constantly seeks to expand its power and funding, without committing itself to any improvements. The pressure accumulates on the democratically elected members of the school board who are caught in between. This is the microcosm of the tension, which leads from the local level to Washington.

The Republic, in principle, was not wedded to any particular place or people. The founders saw it as the form of government and society that was the most natural and moral. It could have been an ideal form of government anywhere. The Republic could have failed in the United States, yet whether it was in existence elsewhere or nowhere, in the eyes of the founders it would still have remained the most just of political orders.

This meant that the regime was unique. It was not connected solely to the people who lived in America. It was theirs if they kept it and belonged to others if they chose to have a regime like this. That made the United States radically different from other nations, which are rooted in a common history, language, culture, and place. For example, France and Japan are deeply tethered to their past. America is rooted in an invention, a form of government designed with a moral and practical end, but not, in principle, rooted in the American people. Hence Franklin's warning. The very concept of the American republic is artificial, unconnected to the past.

The regime is called the United States. The country is called

America. The regime and the country are linked by the country's accepting the principles of the regime. It need not do so in order for America, the country, to exist. Americans could have chosen to switch to a different form of government—a monarchy, for example—and the country would have remained America. But we would no longer have been the United States, in the full institutional and moral meaning of the term. The United States of America is the place where the principles of the regime govern the country. This is a very different understanding from what exists in most other countries, and it has profound, and sometimes not recognized, consequences.

You can say that you are a citizen of the United States, but you cannot say I am a "United Statian." The language doesn't permit it. Your natural relationship is to America, your homeland. Saying you are American is easy. But your love of the land and of the people, and your relationship to the United States, are very different things. One of the constant challenges of the Republic is to keep the two aligned, for our natural inclination is to love our home, and loving the Republic is an intellectual exercise. The two need not be one, but the American founding is designed to make certain that there is no unbridgeable distinction. Mostly it works. When it doesn't, there is tension.

Shortly after the Declaration of Independence was signed, Thomas Jefferson, John Adams, and Benjamin Franklin formed a committee to design a great seal for the United States. Given that the United States had been plunged into war by the signing of the declaration, this would not have seemed a priority. What these three men knew, however, was that the United States was a moral project and moral projects require icons, things that define the moral mission and carry with them a sense of the sacred. It took years to produce the Great Seal. In 1782, Charles Thomson, secretary of the Continental Congress, was asked to take this project to conclusion. He did, and the final product now rests in several places, as sacred in

American life as the Republic's principles. The most important place you will find it is nearest to the hearts of Americans: the dollar bill.

Inventing the government was the preface to inventing a nation. Governments can be machines, but nations have to accommodate the actual lives of people. People don't live abstract lives. They live real ones, within nations, and those nations give them a sense of who they are. Partly it has to do with the government. Partly it has to do with the principles of the nation, the things that tell us what kinds of people we are and ought to be. There can be weighty tomes written on this subject, but Jefferson, Adams, and Franklin provided the nation with a great seal that was to be a prism through which we looked at ourselves and that explains why we behave as we do. The Great Seal is symbolic and the symbols must be decoded. But in those symbols, we can find what they thought Americans should be and what citizenship in the United States must be.

We should take the Great Seal seriously because of the three men who called it into being. They not only were among the most extraordinary members of a group of extraordinary men but also represented all the major factions of the revolution. Jefferson was a democrat. Adams was a Federalist. Franklin was an iconoclast, and perhaps best represented the American spirit. He was a serious man. He was not a sober one. Franklin was a party of one and represented the people who loved the country, but he understood that decency required humor. It is amazing that three minds such as these—a philosophical genius, a legal genius, and a genius at living well—were able to share a single vision of who we were and who we must remain.

On the front of the seal is the eagle, said to represent the strength of America. Benjamin Franklin actually objected to the choice of the eagle, explaining his rationale in a letter to his daughter:

For my own part I wish the Bald Eagle had not been chosen the Representative of our Country. He is a Bird of bad moral

Character. He does not get his Living honestly. You may have seen him perched on some dead Tree near the River, where, too lazy to fish for himself, he watches the Labour of the Fishing Hawk; and when that diligent Bird has at length taken a Fish, and is bearing it to his Nest for the Support of his Mate and young Ones, the Bald Eagle pursues him and takes it from him.

Franklin is said to have preferred the turkey, a more honest bird. He most likely couldn't tolerate the cliché of an eagle. Franklin was being funny, but he was also making the serious point that symbols matter.

On the banner, next to the eagle are the words *E pluribus unum,* meaning "From many, one." It was said at the time to refer to the thirteen colonies, the many joining together and being one. Over time, however, history has given a different meaning to the phrase. Once the waves of immigration washed across the United States, the motto was used to refer to the manner in which the many cultures that had come to America had become one nation. It is unlikely that the founders ever envisioned the diversity of immigration, although the Constitution clearly anticipated it because it set the rules for naturalization. The Scots-Irish—Protestant Scots from Ireland who arrived after the English—were loathed as violent and unassimilable. It is an old story in the history of American immigration. The Great Seal is fixed in principle. It evolves in practice. Out of many, one, turned out to be the basis on which the American people were founded, but never easily. Here we are, 250 years later, and the principle of immigration still tears at the nation.

But the original meaning of *E pluribus unum* pointed at another, deadly problem that led to the Civil War. It is easy to forget how different the colonies were from each other and how aware they were of their differences. Rhode Island differed from South Carolina in geography, customs, and social order. Those differences endure today, but as a shadow of what they once were. *E pluribus unum* was chosen as a motto not because the new states had much in common but because to some extent they regarded each other as strange and exotic foreigners. Today we may not be strangers, but a New Yorker is frequently exotic to a Texan, and vice versa. The tension endures.

On the back of the seal is an unfinished pyramid, an interesting choice for an emerging modern country in a time when pyramids had not been built for many centuries. But its symbolism is powerful. A pyramid is a massive undertaking, involving the wealth and resources and labor of a nation. It is a unifying principle. The pyramid ties the Republic for which it stands and the people who built it into one. It tells us that the Republic is not simply a concept but the product of a people, and that ties the Republic to a nation.

The seal also signifies that the Republic is a work in progress and must evolve through the intense labor of Americans. The people endlessly build the pyramid on the land. A pyramid has a shape that compels the work to proceed in a certain way. You make the brick, you make the mortar, you lay the brick in an endless cycle. The pyramid gives labor its form and its predictability. Labor also has its moments of crisis and of success. This describes what American life will be like.

Above the pyramid are the words *Annuit coeptis,* meaning, "He has favored our undertaking." "He" is assumed to be God. Yet it was decided not to use the word "God." There is a great controversy in America between those who argue the United States is a Christian country and others who claim that it is completely secular. The creators of the seal clearly understood this issue. Whether they compromised or whether they were unanimous, there is no mention of Christ or even God in either the Declaration of Independence or the Constitution. Yet there is a clear reference to something beyond humanity who judges and favors the undertaking, a providence, as it is called in the Declaration of Independence. The founders could have referred directly to Christ, or they could have avoided any reference to the divine. They did neither. They did not simply embrace the secularism of the Enlightenment nor the religiosity of England. They refused to name the providential force, but they made it clear that there was one. The ambiguity was, I think, deliberate. It developed a creative tension that endures.

Beneath the pyramid is the third motto on the seal: *Novus ordo seclorum,* which means a "new order of the ages." This is how the founders viewed the founding of the United States. It was not simply a new form of government but a dramatic shift in the history of humanity. That was radical enough. However, Charles Thomson, who crafted the phrase, said that what it represented was "the beginning of the new American era." The most reasonable way to interpret this is that a new age has begun, and America would be at the center of the new age. There was nothing reasonable about this assertion at the time. In fact, it was downright preposterous. America was in its infancy, sharing a world filled with countries that had existed and evolved for centuries, if not millennia. The age that Europe had defined was far from over, and a new age, transcending the European age, was not yet visible. Nevertheless, the founders saw a new age arising, the American age, and they embossed it on the Great Seal.

The Great Seal gives us a superb sense of what the founders envisioned, corrupted as it was by slavery, which I will discuss later. They saw the founding of the United States as a new era, filled with unending effort, but effort shaped toward a prescribed and logical end. It would be an era acknowledging something divine, but an unspecified divinity. They imagined greatness, the sacred, and a nation built on the foundations of work. The seal gives us a sense of what the founders wanted but not a precise one. The mottoes give a sense of America's trajectory and ends. Knowing the destination, we can chart our route and from there predict the dangers we will face and the opportunities that will greet us.

The founders believed that a handful of people, perched on the western edge of the Atlantic Ocean, could not only defeat a great global empire like Britain but also build a nation that could reshape the world. Therefore, the discussion naturally moves from the Great Seal to the revolution. In a sense, the American Revolution was not directed against England alone. It was directed against the European age that had begun in 1492. The Americans viewed the European age as founded on oppression and inequality. European nations believed these values to be the natural order of things. Against this order, the founders posed not merely liberty and equality but also the domination of nature. The Industrial Revolution was in its infancy, but its basic principle was already visible. It was the domination of nature by reason and technology. So much of American history turned on science and its spawn, technology. When we look at Ben Franklin or Thomas Jefferson, we see that the founders had a vision transcending the nation.

It is worth pausing to remember that two of the three men who commissioned the seal were inventors. Both Jefferson and Franklin invented many things, from a lightweight plow to the lightning rod. Jefferson was a superb architect, leaving behind Monticello in Virginia, the extraordinary home he created—the home that featured his invention of the dumbwaiter. When I say that the regime was invented, I am therefore saying that it was invented by men who were lifelong inventors. They were technologists. They tried to create things that would manage nature and ease human existence. Invention was not only part of the regime. It was built into American culture. Jefferson and Franklin questioned all political premises. They also questioned all things and how to improve them. This inventiveness can be seen throughout American history, from farm implements to smartphones.

This inventiveness was coupled with a sense of urgency. People came to the United States to live better than they had lived at home.

An immigrant settling in New York or Minnesota with empty pockets needed and wanted to move quickly. Time was of the essence, and time remained of the essence in American culture.

It was a combination of urgency and technology that drove the United States forward. In every generation, there were inventions that changed the way men lived, and this created a cycle of transformation for society as a whole. That cycle included the inevitable failures and disappointments that are inherent in technology, whether in the design of houses, the management of electricity, or the invention of government. Once invented, the inventions had to be reinvented to deal with new challenges and new possibilities.

Let's consider a phrase in the Declaration of Independence that is so common to the American mind that its incredible idiosyncrasy is ignored. The founders speak of three rights: the right to life, liberty, and the pursuit of happiness. The source for this phrase was John Locke, a British philosopher who spoke of "the right to life, liberty, and property." The founders changed "property" to "the pursuit of happiness." They deliberately chose this term, which is both difficult to understand and at the core of American culture.

Technology and invention are always, in some sense, tied to happiness. The computer, the automobile, the telephone, and so on made working, traveling, and communicating easier. They opened up possibilities that had not been there before. Think of the advances in medicine. Medical breakthroughs don't eliminate death, but they might keep it at bay for a while, and that makes us happy. So technology and happiness are intimately linked in American life, to the point that technology is at times a substitute for other types of happiness, such as love and the divine. Americans value those things, but they love cutting-edge technology with a different but real passion.

Any discussion of the invention of the American government, therefore, must turn to invention in general and from there to happiness. The founders knew that, which is why the Declaration of

Independence declared the pursuit of happiness an inherent right. And that creates a puzzle.

The pursuit of happiness defines American culture. It is not that there aren't other paths, such as duty and love and charity. But they all orbit around the central core of pursuing an end, happiness, which is a highly individual concept and can be defined in as many ways as there are people. All are invited to establish their own definition of happiness. If we think of it in this way, the definition of liberty becomes clear. Liberty is the precondition to the pursuit of happiness. Liberty is the freedom to define one's own happiness.

Happiness is the emotional engine powering the United States. It is the only country to make the pursuit of happiness a fundamental right. But with happiness comes disappointment, just as with technology comes obsolescence. The regime is a machine, a novel tool for getting things done. But as what needs to get done changes, the structure of the regime must change as well. And changing state institutions has traditionally been painful and intimately tied to war. We will turn to that in part 2. First, we need to examine the American land, the thing that is permanent, yet in the United States has changed and been reinvented many times.

2

The Land—a Place
Called America

The man who named the Western Hemisphere was Martin Waldseemüller. He was a German mapmaker who in 1507 was drawing a map of the new world. Amerigo Vespucci, an Italian explorer sailing for the Portuguese, was the first to realize that Columbus had not visited India but had encountered a new landmass. Vespucci sent his notes to Waldseemüller, who he knew was creating a map. Waldseemüller had to name the place depicted on the map, and the name couldn't be India, regardless of what Columbus had thought. Waldseemüller decided to call the hemisphere "America" in honor of Amerigo Vespucci, and such was the origin of the name.

The hemisphere had no name before America. Those who had lived there had names for themselves and others they knew of, but they had no need to name a hemisphere that was, to them, their entire world. The natives of the Eastern Hemisphere had no name for that hemisphere either. In giving the Western Hemisphere a name, Waldseemüller reinvented the world. He asserted that the world consisted of two hemispheres, and in naming it after an Italian—a name that is used to this day—he gave it a European identity.

The name America would come to define the hemisphere, and

with that redefinition it became increasingly European rather than something the natives still owned. The geography stayed the same; mountains and rivers move over eons, but the relationship between that geography and those who inhabited it was transformed. As railroads and vast cities developed, they changed not just the landscape of the country but also how people conceived of its geography. Diverting rivers in order to grow crops in the desert gives both a different understanding of geography and a different sense of what is possible. This is why I would assert that while all humans in some way reinvent geography, Americans have been far more ambitious (or egregious) in inventing and reinventing American geography. It is this reinvention that has allowed the United States to experience explosive development, and to evolve so quickly as a powerful country.

Just as the regime was invented, so too was the land—or at least the relationship of the land to those who came to settle. In each generation and in each wave of immigrants, the meaning of the mountains and soil and rivers changed. It was a vast country and underpopulated compared with Europe or Asia. The Europeans became Americans and swept aside the natives. In doing so, they opened the door to inventing and reinventing the land. In a way the land was as artificial as the regime.

Settling North America

America consists of two large islands barely connected by a land bridge at Panama. The two islands have very different geographies. The most striking features of the southern island are the vast rainforest called the Amazon and the mountains along the west, the Andes. The most striking feature of the northern island is the vast plain between two mountain ranges, the Rockies and the Appalachians, and the complex of rivers that flow from the mountains, through the plains to the Gulf of Mexico. The southern island was rich in gold and silver. The northern, except for Mexico, was rich in land that could be farmed.

The reason the Europeans came at all, and when they did, was a desire to reach India and the East Indies. The famous Silk Road went west from India and China, bringing products to Europe via the Mediterranean. In the mid-fifteenth century, the road was interdicted by the rise of an Islamic empire, the Ottomans, centered on Turkey. They first blocked the road and then dramatically increased the tax on goods passing through. The Europeans depended on the Silk Road for goods, but the Ottomans had priced those goods to painful levels.

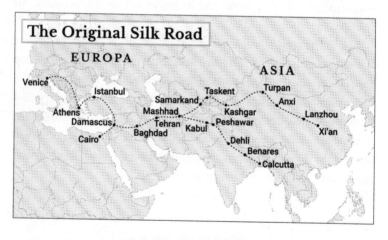

Whoever found a route to India that took them around the Ottomans would solve Europe's problem and become wealthy. The Portuguese succeeded first, going around Africa. The Spaniards, delayed by their war with the Muslims, sought a route toward the west. It was a good move in theory. In practice, it failed because the Spaniards didn't know that the Western Hemisphere blocked their way.

What at first appeared a failure turned out to be a fabulous success, at least for Spain. The currents and winds from Iberia provided a highway from there to the Caribbean and from the Caribbean to the east coast of South America and later to the west coast. The Portuguese arrived first in force and therefore claimed Brazil, where they created great plantations built on the concept of enslaved Indians and slaves brought in from Africa. But it was the Spaniards who followed the Portuguese and who had to continue past Brazil to the west coast who won the great prize. The Inca Empire, in today's Peru, controlled fabulously productive gold and silver mines, and it had already mined a vast trove of both, which the Spanish desired.

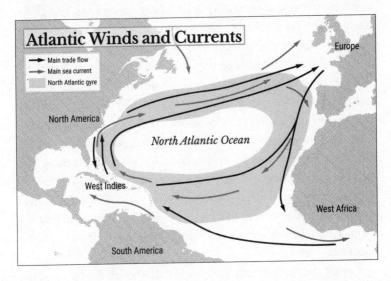

The currents and winds made it harder to get to North America, and there was less obvious wealth to exploit. It seemed that North America was of little value. The Spanish, in particular, did not come to settle but did come to steal, and therefore the Spanish focused on South America, filled with gold and silver. Spain was in Europe, and Europe was filled with enemies. The Spanish needed large armies and couldn't afford to let their population emigrate. The same was true of Portugal. They were content to destroy and enslave Native empires, use these slaves on plantations, and plunder their gold and silver. This left a thin layer of officials and adventurers dominating the Native population. It was extraordinary that a handful of adventurers conquered entire nations. They had superior technology, but the truth behind the victory was the diseases they brought from Europe.

In the short run, Portugal and Spain were the winners, but not in the long run. They avoided North America due to difficult currents, winds, and weather, and once they arrived, the explorers found the Atlantic coast racked by storms and inhabited by Indians who were not easily cowed. But North America had two things the south didn't have. One was animals with luxurious furs, particularly beaver. These were expensive and surprisingly profitable for the French, who also did little settling but much trapping and trading. The French saw North America's possibilities in a vast wilderness, populated by Indian nations and the beaver. The French established a settlement at Quebec, but like Spain, France was not interested in a vast outflow of settlers when it needed manpower for its armies. But there were profits to be made in trapping and trading fur. And because trading was more efficient than trapping, the French developed close commercial and political relations with the Indian nations—without having to devote significant resources to battling them. That relationship was the foundation of their power in North America.

The second thing North America had that South America did not was rich farming land in vast amounts and a river system to bring the produce to ports. It was the English who realized that North America had, in the long term, the most valuable prize. England was an island, and the English did not need massive numbers of soldiers. They could spare settlers, and the land welcomed them. In the end, it was the English who outstripped the Iberians, replaced the Spanish navy in the North Atlantic, and reshaped the geography of North America. Migration was a difficult process with a high cost that never ended. But it was the English migration, the English settlement, that transformed North America into the center of the global system.

Settlement began with the first English colony, founded on Roanoke Island in today's North Carolina in 1587, less than a century after Columbus's voyage. It failed catastrophically. After Roanoke was settled, a war broke out between England and Spain, and for three years no supplies were delivered to a colony that was far from self-sufficient. When the war ended and the supply ships returned, there was no settlement to be found.

No one is certain what happened to the Roanoke Colony. The best evidence is that having received no supplies, and unable to support themselves, the settlers had taken refuge among friendly Indians. The Indian nations, like the Europeans, were constantly at war with each other. Indications are that the Indian nation giving the settlers refuge was attacked by a hostile Indian nation that massacred both. It was a lonely death in a faraway place.

The English waited for twenty years before colonizing again, this time at Jamestown, on the coast of what is now Virginia. It was the first colony on the eastern coast of North America to survive. The colony was owned by the Virginia Company and financed by investors seeking large returns on their investment. The settlers were primarily gentlemen adventurers looking to make their fortunes through sweat equity. There were other members of the colony, particularly craftsmen and laborers who had smaller ambitions. It was a place where immigrants could seek their fortunes but where the English class structure remained intact and defined what fortunes could be sought. Jamestown presaged the future of America. It was funded by investors, looking for a substantial return from the ambitions and efforts of others. Jamestown combined the British aristocracy with the American venture capitalist.

Other new European colonies were established over the following decades. Santa Fe, today's capital of New Mexico, was founded in

1607, by Spaniards. They were searching for more gold, and there were always myths and lies about fortunes to be made in the north of Mexico. The Spaniards found no gold but learned that the deserts and mountains separating today's Mexico from the rest of North America were daunting. The Mexicans had to cross deserts. The English had to cross the ocean. It was not obvious that Jamestown would trump Santa Fe for several centuries. Then, a year after Santa Fe, in 1608, Quebec was established along the St. Lawrence River. It was a time for founding. This was the year in which contemporary history truly began with the competition of three great European cities: London, Paris, and Madrid.

Twelve years later, Plymouth was founded in what is now Massachusetts. Plymouth Colony is better known to Americans, and many believe it was the first English colony. It was the second, after Jamestown, and, if one includes Roanoke, the third. Like Jamestown, Plymouth Colony was funded by a venture capital group, this one called the Merchant Adventurers. Most of the settlers weren't Pilgrims but adventurers like those who settled Jamestown. The Pilgrims didn't run the colony. The Merchant Adventurers did. And the colony was divided between the religious and the adventurers, called Strangers. The Mayflower Compact was a tricky piece of work. The majority of men were Strangers. But if one counts women and children who could not vote, the Pilgrims were in the majority and set rules that outvoted the adventurers, causing substantial tensions.

Five years after Plymouth, the Dutch founded the New Amsterdam colony in what is now southern Manhattan. Much like the French, the Dutch came to trade, not to settle. They raised seed capital from the Dutch West India Company and founded a trading post. The Hudson River valley divided the Appalachian Mountains, giving the Dutch access to northern and western New York and the Great Lakes. The region was filled with beavers, which the Europeans highly valued for men's top hats. Trappers captured beavers and traded with the Indians for them, then sold them at a trading post near today's Albany. The pelts were transported to New Amsterdam, from where they were shipped and sold in Europe. New Amsterdam harbor became the main link between North America and Europe. Then, in 1664, England seized it and renamed it New York.

These colonies foretold an American reality. Each colony was a corporate undertaking owned by investors taking risks in the hope of making substantial amounts of money. Investors were indifferent to how they made money, or with whom. If the money was made from plantations built on slavery, or on trading posts securing furs, or on small farms, it was all the same. If Plymouth Colony wanted to pretend that it was controlled by Protestant dissenters, that was fine by the Merchant Adventurers group, so long as there was a satisfactory return on investment. Ultimate control was in the hands of the investors, and the pressure was on the settlers to generate a return.

Living in North America

The Atlantic and the Appalachians defined the colonies. The distance between the two shaped not just the commercial but the moral nature of the colonies. South of Pennsylvania, the Appalachians were over two hundred miles from the Atlantic coast. There was flat, fertile land in abundance, for large commercial plantations. North of Pennsylvania, the distance from the mountains to the oceans was much less, the soil was rocky and hilly, and the winters were long. There was room only for family farms, craftsmen, merchants, and bankers. In the South, large plantations needed cheap labor. In the North, a helper or two was all that was required. This distinction defined American history, slave and free, confederate and unionist. It was there from the beginning. Geography made slavery desirable and profitable in the South. In the North, geography made slavery uneconomical. Thus, we see the geographic foundation of the institutional and moral crisis that tore the United States apart centuries later.

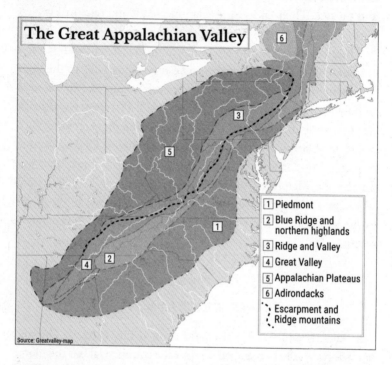

The Great Appalachian Valley

1. Piedmont
2. Blue Ridge and northern highlands
3. Ridge and Valley
4. Great Valley
5. Appalachian Plateaus
6. Adirondacks
   Escarpment and Ridge mountains

Source: Greatvalley-map

There were different Americas reflecting the two founding colonies. The South, the area where the distance from the Atlantic to the Appalachians was large enough to accommodate plantations, generated men whose manners, if not beliefs, reflected the English nobility that the adventurers at Jamestown hoped to emulate. In the North, the Calvinist asceticism of Plymouth Colony created a colony that combined a commitment to commerce with a deep moralism. The two regions created different types of leaders and pointed to a deep split in the future republic. Consider two of the leaders of the revolution.

George Washington was the great-grandson of John Washington, who immigrated to Virginia in 1656. John's father was born in England to a royalist family. When the royalists lost power, John's father, a clergyman of some note, was stripped of all his possessions. His son sailed as second officer on a ship bound for America. Having seen his family lose everything in England, he was a gentleman, but a poor one. He married well and made the best of it in his new circumstances. He traded in land and bought land to grow and export tobacco. He prospered, living the life of an English nobleman without titles but with slaves. This was not an exceptional story for the time.

John Adams was born to a Puritan family in Massachusetts. His father was a deacon in the church, and his mother's father was a physician. Adams's ambition ran to the law and the professional life without any desire to emulate English nobility. There were opportunities in merchant banking and shipbuilding. There was wealth to be had in New England, but it was the life of what the English called the middle class.

The settlers were all English, but they came with different ambitions. Some came to live the luxurious lives of English noblemen, living in grand houses and, lacking serfs, being served by African slaves. Others came to America to live the solid middle-class lives of ministers, lawyers, and merchants. Most came here to make a living working with their hands. Like millions after them, they came for jobs that valued their craft or for a piece of land they could farm. Most had modest hopes, simply something better than they had where they were born. Others dreamed of obtaining the wealth of a merchant, honestly earned and kept. And others dreamed of the nobility denied them in England.

The division wasn't just the work of the Appalachians. It was also the work of rivers. South of New York, all rivers flowed from the Appalachians east into the Atlantic. In the North, they ran from north to south, connecting the states. Southern rivers did not unite southern states. The rivers didn't provide transportation between states, and roads were hard and expensive to build. In the South, each colony was distinct and would remain that way.

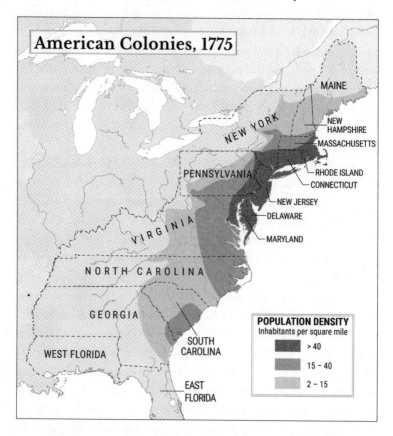

American Colonies, 1775

MAINE

NEW YORK

NEW HAMPSHIRE

MASSACHUSETTS

PENNSYLVANIA

RHODE ISLAND

CONNECTICUT

NEW JERSEY

DELAWARE

VIRGINIA

MARYLAND

NORTH CAROLINA

GEORGIA

SOUTH CAROLINA

WEST FLORIDA

EAST FLORIDA

POPULATION DENSITY
Inhabitants per square mile

> 40

15 – 40

2 – 15

There was another factor that isolated the southern colonies from each other and from the North. In addition to poor transportation, the large physical size of the colonies, and sparse population, the South produced different products than the North—tobacco and cotton. These two main products of the plantation were sold primarily to England, not to the North. The South would join the revolution, but it would have less of a sense of being American than of being distinct colonies allied with other colonies. The idea of a unified nation under a single government ran counter to the geographic reality of most of the South. The same wasn't true in New England, where distances were shorter, population denser, and distinctions smaller. The idea of a powerful national government was easier to grasp in the North. The fundamental issue was not yet the relation of north and south, but rather the relation of the colonies to England.

The Origins of the United States

In 1754, the Seven Years' War broke out. It involved virtually all European powers and raged throughout the world. The war consisted of two alliances, one led by the British, the other by the French, and the triggering issue was the status of Silesia. Another of the issues was the British colonies in North America. The French feared that they would be expelled from North America by the British, and Britain feared that the French and their Indian allies would seize Britain's colonies. The real issue, however, was whether Britain or France would dominate Europe and the world.

In North America the strategic issue was control of the Ohio Territory, a region west of the Appalachians whose heart was the Ohio River. The French wanted to get rid of British power—such as it was—west of the Appalachians. But British power was east of the Appalachians, and therefore France had to cross the Appalachians, overwhelm the colonies, and thereby expel the British from North America. The Appalachians became the line of battle.

For the British, this was a small part of a global war. For the colonists, everything was at stake. The colonists raised militias to block the French and the Indians. One of these was commanded

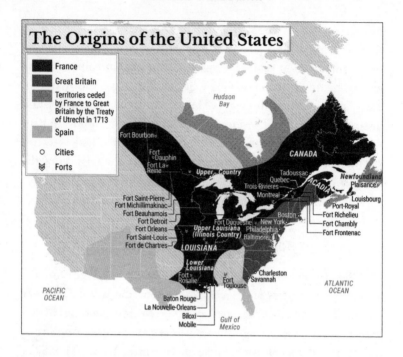

by Colonel George Washington, then twenty-two years old. The colonists were following the English tradition that class was more important than experience. Washington was not the worst commander the colonists had, but at twenty-two he needed the almost impassable Appalachians to help him out. The colonists held the Appalachian line by themselves. The British had more important uses for their troops.

After a time, the British did send troops, commanded by General Edward Braddock. Braddock didn't understand the Appalachians. The English had fought their wars on the north European plain, a very flat surface. There straight rows and columns of soldiers fought and maneuvered in large formations. This was how gentlemen fought.

Gentlemanly fighting was impossible in the Appalachians, with their rugged hills and heavy woods. Here, men fought alone or in small groups, hiding behind rocks and trees and setting up ambushes. Stealth and initiative were the keys to success. Mass and order were impossible. The Indians, of course, knew this well, as did the French, having learned from the Indians. The colonists' knowledge was divided between the gentry who wanted to emulate the English and the poorer men who had hunted for food in the mountains and thought their social betters quite insane. Washington's virtue is that he grasped the reality of the battlefield.

For Braddock and his officers, the manner in which the colonials fought was undignified. Wars were about not just winning but winning with grace and style. Therefore the British treated the American troops and officers with contempt. The Americans fought like barbarians. For men like Washington, who saw himself as English, an officer and a gentleman, the contempt was unbearable. It reminded them that in the eyes of the British aristocrats, they were nothing of the sort. This was the moment when the breach between Britain and the colonies opened up. Braddock turned out to be a catastrophe as a general in North America, leading his men into disaster. Yet, in spite of the British defeat, the colonials were still seen as lesser men.

The war ignited the colonists' anger at the British, particularly among the more influential classes. Out of that anger came a profound realization. It was the moment when the colonials realized that they were not English but Americans. A new sense of "nation" began to emerge from this war and from the Appalachians.

The struggle for the Appalachians changed the American character and began to shape the nation. For all the colonists might have wished to look like the British aristocracy, they did not share the aristocratic belief that their right to rule had nothing to do with their competence or achievement. For Americans, who struggled for what they had, achievement was everything. Even a third-generation aristocrat like Washington knew that. He was an aristocrat in a very American way. British contempt forged colonial America. It was the colonists' observation of the British officer corps during the fighting in the Appalachians that convinced them that victory in a revolutionary war was possible. The British would eventually surrender to the colonials at Yorktown, but they actually lost the colonies years earlier at Fort Duquesne in Pennsylvania, where Braddock was crushed. They were defeated in a battle they should have won. It was a lesson the Americans didn't forget.

Braddock's defeat opened a cultural gulf between the colonies and the British. The Americans realized that the British didn't understand America. They realized that America was a very different place. In a way this was more of a shock to the southern states that patterned themselves after the British social order than to New England, but to all it drove home that the British pattern of history would not be the American pattern, and that opened the door to a deep rethinking of what America was.

The men who signed the Declaration of Independence were part of the generation that lived through the Seven Years' War. Almost all the signers were born between 1720 and 1740, and the United States had changed dramatically during their lives. In 1720, there were about 466,000 Europeans living in the colonies. By 1740, that number had risen to about 900,000, and by 1776 there were about 2.5 million. The colonists' population was about the same size as that of Portugal, a mature continental power. This generation lived with one eye on the Atlantic and one eye on the mountains. And some, like Thomas Jefferson, looked beyond the Appalachians.

American Rivers

America could not survive as a long and narrow strip of land along the East Coast. The British hadn't forgotten the colonies they lost, and the United States could not easily defend itself. It had a small navy, and it couldn't move its forces around easily. The problem was its rivers. They ran from west to east, from the mountains to the ocean, for the most part. Therefore it was difficult to rapidly move troops north and south. The direction the rivers flowed made the United States weak. It made the lack of strategic depth unbearable. But on the other side of the Appalachians, there was not only depth but also an extraordinary system of rivers. Depth would solve many problems.

The engine driving American expansion begins at Lake Itasca, a very small lake in northern Minnesota, about one hundred miles from Canada. It is beautiful and isolated country, and the lake measures about two square miles. A twenty-foot-wide stream flows out of it, toward the south. The Chippewa Indians had called the stream Mississippi, in English "large river." As the Mississippi flows south, thirteen major rivers flow into it, along with seventy-seven lesser rivers. Most of these rivers are navigable, and they all flow south past the city of New Orleans (founded in 1718) and into the Gulf of Mexico and the global oceans.

Jefferson had written that "France possessing herself of Louisiana . . . is the embryo of a tornado which will burst on the countries on both shores of the Atlantic and involve in its effects their highest destinies." Jefferson foresaw that whoever controlled Louisiana would likely be the most powerful nation in the world. He proved to be right. Napoleon's desperate need for cash, and Jefferson's yearning for Louisiana, gave the United States the key to global power for $15 million, a staggeringly small amount even then. Napoleon was a great soldier. Jefferson understood grand strategy.

For Thomas Jefferson, this region would not only give the United States strategic depth and security. It would allow settlers to own and farm their own land. But most important, the surplus they produced could be shipped south on barges to New Orleans, put on board oceangoing freighters, and sold to Europe. And that sale would create a prosperous America built on well-to-do farmers, free and equal. That wasn't possible east of the Appalachians, and west of them, in the Northwest Territories, where the European threat still existed. If the United States could take the land west to the Rockies, the United States would be secure and would become a great power.

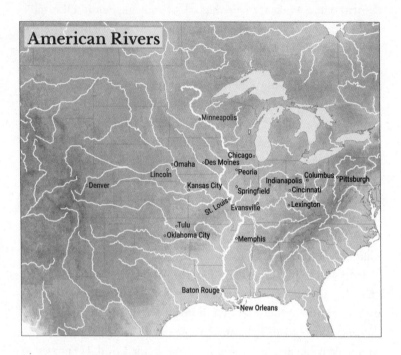

To understand what Jefferson created, it's important to understand a bill passed by Congress in 1787: the Northwest Ordinance. The Northwest Territories was a region between the Appalachians and the Mississippi that the United States had seized from Britain in the revolution. The ordinance laid the legal groundwork for reshaping the West. The ordinance established that the Northwest Territories would, as its population grew, be divided into new states and not just be colonies. It said that the territory and states created would prohibit slavery. It allowed Revolutionary War veterans to acquire land, at almost no cost, that they owned outright, free to sell or trade. They were not to be serfs. And finally, and perhaps most extraordinarily, every state created out of the territory would be required to found a state university, by selling land to support it. In 1804, the first, Ohio University, was founded. All of that would apply to the Louisiana Territory and create a land of yeomen farmers and obligatory universities. And those universities would revolutionize America.

Jefferson also had a political reason for westward expansion:

The larger our association, the less will it be shaken by local passions; and in any view is it not better that the opposite bank of the Mississippi should be settled by our own brethren and children than by strangers of another family?

According to Jefferson, there was a strategic reason for the purchase but also a vital political reason: the larger the country, the greater the stability, because local passions were more divisive in a small land than in a large one. There was also an economic reason. The Louisiana Territory contained some of the richest farmland in the world. It could drive the American economy forward while containing the centrifugal forces economic growth unleashes. Jefferson was trying to answer the threat of fragmentation and also create an economic foundation that would cushion the cycles the United States would face.

The Louisiana Purchase would wind up being the engine that propelled the United States to global power a century later. It also created the force that would end the first cycle in American history, with western settlers challenging the power of eastern bankers and plantation owners. If the regime set in motion the moral and political foundations of American power, the Louisiana Purchase drove the economic forces that would systematically, over more than two centuries, transform the United States in a series of cycles.

The War with the Indians

Many have debated what to call the nations native to North America. Obviously, the best terms are the ones used by the natives themselves, which were the names of their own nations. But it is also necessary to have a term that speaks of these peoples as a whole. The term "Indian" stems from a navigational error by Columbus. The term "Native American" would name them after an Italian. The term the Canadians favor is "First Nation," which suffers from being untrue. They had been in the Western Hemisphere for millennia and had, like humans everywhere, made war on each other and occupied each other's land. The nations present when the Europeans came were hardly first nations. The naming issue points out the complexity of the moral dilemma. I use the name Indian because it is no less appropriate than the other choices, and it is in common use.

North America was populated by Indian nations, and the early history of the United States was intricately intertwined with the history of the Indians. In Mexico and Peru, the Aztecs and Incas had been stunned and their political systems rapidly destroyed by the Spanish conquistadors. It was different in North America. First, there were many nations, and the collapse of one did not mean the collapse of others. There were many nations with different languages and cultures. These nations had been surrounded by foreigners well before the Europeans came, such as the Toltecs or the Apache. They understood war and diplomacy battling the Comanche or joining the Iroquois confederation.

Foreign powers were part of North American culture, and the arrival of a new one, even given the odd appearance and new technologies of the Europeans, did not cause a psychological collapse. The Iroquois, for example, led a complex confederation of nations, as well as nations that had been subjugated. New technologies like iron and gunpowder might have been novel, but given the number of Europeans and their inability to understand the terrain, it was not surprising that the Iroquois and other natives not only didn't crumble but tended to defeat the Europeans in most early hostile encounters.

The major groupings looked like this in 1800:

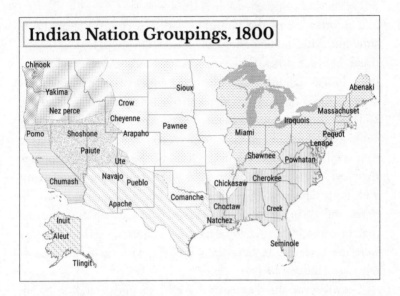

Indian Nation Groupings, 1800

The map of Indian North America was like the map of any region of the Eastern Hemisphere. The continent was divided between groups that were foreign to each other and frequently hostile. There were subgroups that resisted the emergence of a powerful central government. The Indians as a whole were no more peaceful nor warlike than any other human group. One safety valve that prevented the land from erupting in war was a large and not fully settled continent that allowed weaker groups to withdraw and survive as nomads. In this it can be compared with central Asia and other parts of Eurasia. The point is that drawing radical distinctions between Indian and European culture is valid on one level. But on the broader level of Indians seeing themselves as distinct nations, engaged in diplomacy and war with neighboring states, the distinction blurs. And as in Europe, these national groupings were frequently torn by dissent. But what's vital to understand is that the Indian nations did not see themselves as one people. They viewed each other as foreigners, and they viewed the Europeans as exotic but in the end comprehensible entities.

The intrusion of the Europeans led to a complex geopolitical situation, with Indian nations allied with European nations, sometimes fighting other European nations and sometimes fighting other Indian nations. Occasionally the alliances lasted a long time; at other times the alliances were quickly betrayed. The Europeans, and then the Americans, had three advantages. First, so long as they could gain a foothold on the continent, they had the ability to bring overwhelming numbers to bear over time. Second, the technology they had was superior in general to what the Indians had. Finally, and most important, the Indians were deeply divided against each other, and allying with a European force meant they could subdue their enemies. A further advantage more devastating than weapons were the diseases the Europeans brought with them and against which the Indians had no defense.

The story of the Comanche is vital to understanding North American history. Pekka Hämäläinen in his award-winning book *The Comanche Empire* chronicles the rise, dominion, and fall of an aggressive Indian empire that existed at the same time as the American movement westward. Until 1700, the Comanche was a small nation living in the canyon lands of New Mexico. At one point they had lived on the plains of the Central Valley, but they were forced out by stronger nations and retreated into the inhospitable canyon lands, where they were safe because no other nation wanted their desolate terrain. As Hämäläinen puts it,

Despite its modest beginnings, the Comanche exodus to the southern plains is one of the key turning points in early

American history. It was a commonplace migration that became a full-blown colonizing project with far-reaching geopolitical, economic, and cultural repercussions. It set off a half-century-long war with the Apaches and resulted in the relocation of Apachería—a massive geopolitical entity in its own right—from the grasslands south of the Río Grande, at the very center of northern New Spain. The Comanche invasion of the southern plains was, quite simply, the longest and bloodiest conquering campaign the American West had witnessed—or would witness until the encroachment of the United States a century and a half later.

Spaniards were already in Mexico at that time, and the Comanche stole, and traded for, the horses they had brought from Europe. The Comanche seized on this new technology, a new way of doing things, and mastered it brilliantly. Comanche braves became incredibly skilled horsemen, more so than the braves from other Indian nations or even the Europeans, who'd had horses for millennia. Horses and historic grievances over their dispossession powered the Comanche's reemergence.

Over the next century, the Comanche left the impoverished canyon lands and moved into the plains east of the Rockies. By the end of the eighteenth century, they had carved out a large empire, driving other nations out of their homelands. Their reach consisted of more than simply the areas they held directly. Comanche raiding parties traveled vast distances all around them, so their area of influence was even greater than the map shows. Mastering the technology of the conquistadors, they themselves became conquistadors.

By the nineteenth century, the Comanche were able to block the movement of European powers. Hämäläinen describes the reality of North America at a time when the movement west of the Appalachians was well under way. He explains his view this way:

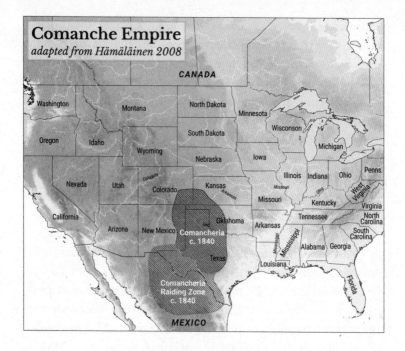

Comanche Empire
adapted from Hämäläinen 2008

CANADA

Washington, Montana, North Dakota, Minnesota, Oregon, Idaho, Wyoming, South Dakota, Wisconsin, Michigan, Nevada, Utah, Colorado, Nebraska, Iowa, Illinois, Indiana, Ohio, Penns., California, Arizona, New Mexico, Kansas, Missouri, Kentucky, West Virginia, Virginia, Comancheria c. 1840, Oklahoma, Arkansas, Tennessee, North Carolina, Texas, Mississippi, Alabama, Georgia, South Carolina, Louisiana, Comancheria Raiding Zone c. 1840, Florida

MEXICO

Instead of perceiving Native policies toward colonial powers simply as strategies of survival, it assumes that Indians, too, could wage war, exchange goods, make treaties, and absorb peoples in order to expand, extort, manipulate, and dominate. . . . [T]he fate of indigenous cultures was not necessarily an irreversible slide toward dispossession, depopulation, and cultural declension.

The Comanche were as genocidal as the Europeans, if not as efficient. They annihilated other nations, both killing and enslaving. Their ruthlessness was deeply feared by other tribes as well as by European settlers. But they also created a complex culture and within their nation were utterly civilized.

The perception that the European settlers simply overwhelmed helpless and spiritual people, or that weak savages were brushed aside, is untrue. In fact, the Europeans defeated capable and sophisticated empire builders, as well as weaker nations. The Comanche and the Iroquois, along with the Aztecs and the Incas, had themselves built significant empires subjecting other nations to their power. They also understood the use of force. The Indians were as capable as the Europeans of all human virtues and vices.

Indian nations occupied North America, which meant that at every stage in the development of the United States, Indians were present as victims, allies, enemies, and conquerors. In the end they lost, partly because of technology and partly for political reasons. Until the very end, in the 1880s, they never formed a general alliance with one another. Some Indian nations found it beneficial to ally with the Americans in order to defeat their more dangerous enemies. Enmity between the Apache and the Comanche ran deeper than hatred for the Americans, particularly at the beginning of the European influx. Like all successful conquerors, including the Romans and the British, the Americans used these divisions in their favor.

It would be interesting to imagine the outcome if all Indians had cooperated and rallied against the Europeans. But that was impossible. The continent was vast and the Indians knew the place where they lived and the immediate neighboring nations, but they did not know places far away. They did not all speak the same language or worship the same gods. And like people everywhere, they feared each other more than they feared the new stranger. With the rise of the United States, the Americans defeated the British, expelled the French, forced the Mexicans far to the south, and crushed the Indian nations and empires, fighting united against an enemy that could not unite against them. The outcome was inevitable.

The Great Valley

I think of all the land between the Appalachians and the Rocky Mountains as part of a single enormous square valley. It is a bit over a thousand miles from east to west and north to south—a million square miles. The valley undulates in some places and is completely flat in other places. But there is hardly a spot where the earth can't be plowed and seeds planted.

For the valley to do what America needs it to do, it must have water. The valley is divided into two parts when it comes to water, making for two very different regions. In the eastern part, the water comes as rain. In the western part, it comes from aquifers, water under the ground.

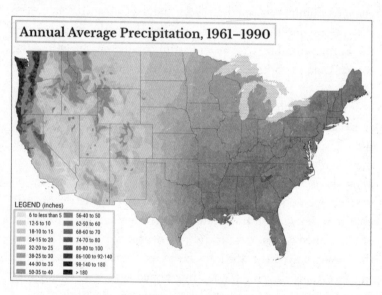

Annual Average Precipitation, 1961–1990

LEGEND (inches)

6 to less than 5	56-40 to 50
12-5 to 10	62-50 to 60
18-10 to 15	68-60 to 70
24-15 to 20	74-70 to 80
32-20 to 25	80-80 to 100
38-25 to 30	86-100 to 92-140
44-30 to 35	98-140 to 180
50-35 to 40	> 180

There is a point where the rainfall declines dramatically. That's a line that runs from Minnesota to central Texas. It is the 100th meridian and starkly divides the continent.

East of this line there were dense forests. When settlers arrived, they would have to clear the land of trees in order to farm, and they used the wood to build log cabins, something of deep symbolism when we think of the generation that crossed the Appalachians, reminding us of Abraham Lincoln. The rain and the forest made for a much denser population in the East, a denseness that exists to this day. You can draw a line north-south through the United States where the rains subside, the trees become scarce, and the population thins out.

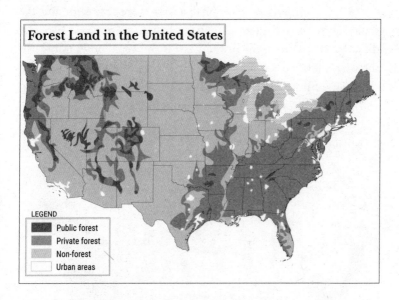

Forest Land in the United States

LEGEND
- Public forest
- Private forest
- Non-forest
- Urban areas

There is still rain to the west of this line, fifteen to twenty inches a year in most parts. But that isn't enough to grow forests. This is the empty prairie of the cowboy myth. The settlers who came here built houses not from wood but from sod, centuries of almost solid remnants of the roots of the grass that covered the region. And they could farm because it was discovered—much to the surprise of earlier explorers—that there were vast water supplies underground that could be tapped by wells.

The lack of wood, and the added effort of drilling wells, meant that this area had (and still has) many fewer people. This has created two sorts of American lives. In the East, well-populated farming communities grew up, and the small towns of American memory were created. In the West, the population had to be more widely spread, so as not to tap the aquifer too intensely in any one area, forcing wells to be drilled deeper and with far more difficulty. The farther west you went, the less likely there was to be farming and the more likely there would be ranching—grazing the grassland. In the West, communities were smaller and more scattered, and the settlers were less reliant on neighbors than on themselves. Two very different ethics emerged. In the East, there were communities. To the west, there was a more solitary life. It created a different political sensibility. In the East, there had to be collaboration. In the West, collaboration brought unnecessary complexity.

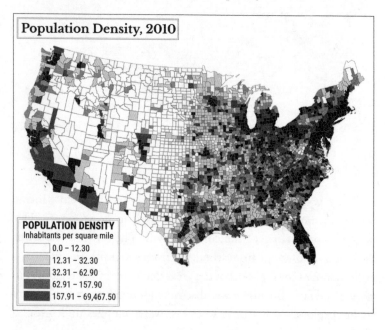

Population Density, 2010

POPULATION DENSITY
Inhabitants per square mile

0.0 – 12.30
12.31 – 32.30
32.31 – 62.90
62.91 – 157.90
157.91 – 69,467.50

Protecting New Orleans

The rivers make the United States possible. New Orleans makes the rivers practical. Without New Orleans, the great valley becomes useless.

Jefferson understood the centrality of New Orleans to American survival:

> There is on the globe one single spot, the possessor of which is our natural and habitual enemy. It is New Orleans, through which the produce of three-eighths of our territory must pass to market, and from its fertility it will ere long yield more than half of our whole produce, and contain more than half our inhabitants. The day that France takes possession of New Orleans fixes the sentence which is to restrain her forever within her low water mark. It seals the union of two nations who in conjunction can maintain exclusive possession of the ocean. From that moment, we must marry ourselves to the British fleet and nation.

Jefferson knew that the loss of New Orleans to France, or any other power including the Spanish or British, would end the dream of American independence. Whoever controlled New Orleans controlled the valley. Whoever controlled the valley controlled the fate of the United States. The United States had to control New Orleans and fought the British, when at the end of the War of 1812 they tried to take it. If they could take New Orleans, they could force the United States back east of the Appalachians. And that would mean that sooner or later they could reverse the outcome of the revolution. Andrew Jackson commanded American forces that defeated the British at New Orleans. Jackson would become an American president, the first one elected from west of the Appalachians. He understood the importance of rivers, because the Cumberland River near his home fed into the Mississippi river system. Jackson understood what was at stake and what his victory meant.

Defeating the British did not end the vulnerability of New Orleans and the Mississippi, at least in Andrew Jackson's mind. The eastern border of Mexico was on the Sabine River, about a hundred miles from the Mississippi and two hundred miles from New Orleans. A Mexican force massed on the Sabine (today's border between Texas and Louisiana) could push eastward and cut the Mississippi and take New Orleans. Mexico was building its population in Texas, including Anglo settlers who became Mexican citizens.

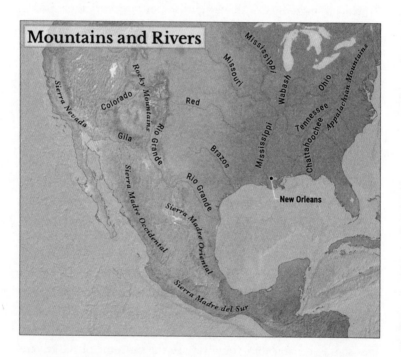

Andrew Jackson was elected president in 1828, and he remained obsessed with New Orleans. He wanted to create a state that was a buffer zone with Mexico. He succeeded, and as a result the Mexicans sent a large force to reverse the rebellion. This was the opposite of what Jackson wanted, because it brought a large military force into Texas, one that could cross the Sabine River. The United States was not ready for a war with Mexico, so it did not intervene militarily. It placed a blocking force east of the Sabine and left it to the Texans to repel the Mexicans.

The road into Texas led to San Antonio, where the Alamo stood. General Santa Anna, commanding the Mexicans, defeated the Texans at the Alamo in 1836 and turned east toward the Sabine. Whether he intended to cross it is unknown. Sam Houston, commanding the Texans, blocked the Mexican advance at San Jacinto, in today's Houston. The Texans defeated the Mexicans, and Texas became an independent country. Seven years later, it became the only state to have entered the United States through a treaty between two equal nations—a cultural legacy that, to this day, gives Texas a unique sense of sovereignty. But in 1845, with Texas becoming a state, the threat to New Orleans seemed to have been eliminated.

The obsession with Mexico continued until the late 1840s, when President Polk launched a war on Mexico that forced it to abandon what is now the American Southwest. That war completed the construction of the continental United States. The founders' pyramid was nearing its geographic completion. Polk, who is insufficiently remembered, was critical in expanding the United States to its full size and setting the foundation for U.S.-Mexican relations as they are today.

The defeat of Mexico integrated the American Southwest, on a line west from Denver to the Pacific. It completed American domination of the Rockies and gave control to the narrow area west of the Rockies to the United States as well. This included harbors at San Diego and San Francisco that opened the door for the United States as a Pacific power.

At this point, the first sketch of the United States was complete. It consisted of the area east of the Appalachians, divided at the Maryland-Pennsylvania border into north and south. There was

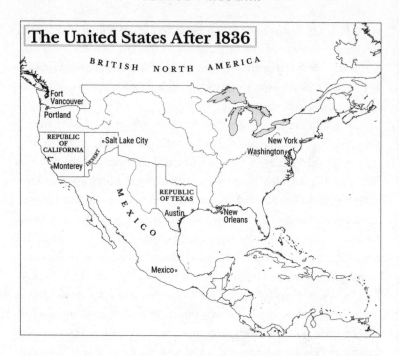

The United States After 1836

the valley between the Appalachians and the Rockies, divided along the tree line running north to south. There were the areas taken from Mexico, divided between the Pacific coast and the desert. Each has developed a different culture. The grasslands are different from the northeast coast. The Mexican regions differed from the wooded East. Each continued to experience life in a different way, but only once—during the Civil War—did the differences turn into bloodshed.

The means Americans used were cleverness, creativity, brutality, and all the other characteristics that defined humanity from its beginning. What is remarkable was the thoroughness of their effort. What began in 1776 was virtually in place a little over seventy years later: a productive continental power stretching from the Atlantic to the Pacific.

No North American power had achieved this before. The Indian nations had a different sense of geography. They feared each other, but they had not learned to fear global forces until it was too late. The Spanish conquerors did not search for fertile land to farm. Their map consisted of gold and silver mines and mythical cities made of gold. The French did not see the continent as having wealth besides the furs the trappers brought in. The British were content with cotton and tobacco flowing to them.

Most Americans never dreamed of what would come. Thomas Jefferson did, and so did Andrew Jackson. Both understood that in creating a continental nation, the United States would discover extraordinary prosperity and a stable democratic order. They also believed that without that continental power, the United States would be destroyed, as were so many nations and settlements that had existed previously in North America. If the United States occupied a sliver or merely a part of the continent, it would not survive. A continent filled with multiple independent nations, such as Europe, would tear itself apart as Europe did.

Therefore, Jefferson and Jackson did what had to be done to create a single continental power. They understood America's geography, and they created a geography in seventy years that would dominate the world.

Contemplating the Whole

George Washington understood the forces that could tear apart the United States and said this in his Farewell Address, delivered in 1796:

> The North, in an unrestrained intercourse with the South, protected by the equal laws of a common government finds in the production of the latter great additional resources of maritime and commercial enterprise and precious materials of

manufacturing industry. The South, in the same intercourse benefitting by the agency of the North, sees its agriculture grow and its commerce expand. Turning partly into its own channels the seamen of the North, it finds its particular navigation invigorated; and, while it contributes, in different ways, to nourish and increase the general mass of the national navigation, it looks forward to the protection of a maritime strength, to which itself is unequally adapted. The East, in a like intercourse with the West, already finds, and in the progressive improvement of interior communications by land and water, will more and more find a valuable vent for the commodities which it brings from abroad, or manufactures at home. The West derives from the East supplies requisite to its growth and comfort, and, what is perhaps of still greater consequence, it must of necessity owe the secure enjoyment of indispensable outlets for its own productions to the weight, influence, and the future maritime strength of the Atlantic side of the Union, directed by an indissoluble community of interest as one nation. Any other tenure by which the West can hold this essential advantage, whether derived from its own separate strength, or from an apostate and unnatural connection with any foreign power, must be intrinsically precarious. . . . In this sense it is that your union ought to be considered as a main prop of your liberty and that the love of the one ought to endear to you the preservation of the other.

Washington divided the country into three parts: north, south, and west. Today we might add to it the far west. He sought to tie these regions together with two things. First, he tried to show the complementary economic interests that bound them together. Second, he made the case that only together could they afford an effective national defense against eastern hemispheric powers. That defense required a strong navy. Divided, one region would fall under the sway of a foreign power, collapsing the entire edifice. For Washington the economic bonds that held the country together also guaranteed the national unity needed for mutual defense.

Washington understood the differences that divided the country, and he feared them. The South and the North had different economies and different moral principles. The West consisted of immigrant settlers—Scots-Irish, Germans, and others who felt only hostility for the eastern English who looked down on them. As the geography of the country was reinvented, so were tensions that threatened to dissolve the country.

The problem was rooted in two things. Institutionally, the United States is one country. But the sensibilities of different regions were deep and constantly caused disunity. Today, the coastal regions, driven by technology and finance, have a common sense of self-worth, justice, and contempt for those who differ. In the industrial Midwest, which was once the booming American heartland, there is a sense of rage at the condition they find themselves in and the disrespect with which their values are treated. There has always been a political division in the country that of course led to the Civil War. But even in less stressful times, like now, the view of Donald Trump is very different in the Northeast and Pacific coast than it is in the South or non-coastal West. And the division was similar in the 1960s. At times of stress and cyclical change, the geography referred to by George Washington reemerges.

There is a fierce unity to America, and simultaneously there are deep differences that turn into mutual contempt at times of stress. This tension actually has a virtue hidden within it. The tension within the country, the radical differences in culture and outlook, actually become a goad driving the country forward but leaving some behind. Thirty-five years after the Civil War, while the South remained mired in the poverty resulting from its defeat, the United States was producing one-half of the world's manufactured products. The Civil War was the most extreme case, but there have always been winners and losers in America. Detroit declines and Atlanta rises. The geography changes, people move, and the United States goes on. In Washington's Farewell Address, he identified the vulnerabilities of the United States and also the fundamental cohesion and resourcefulness that would guide it.

3

The American People

Most nations define nationality in terms of shared history, culture, and values. The American people had none of these. They did not even share a language. Rather they came as aliens, having nothing in common. But an odd evolution took place. The immigrants came to have two cultures. One was the culture of their families, recalling their past. The other was the culture of the nation into which they merged without disappearing. The American culture was defined by this dichotomy, and hence the "American people" is a very real—but artificial—construct.

It was not only immigration that invented the American people. The American people invented themselves. They found themselves with an unprecedented regime and an extraordinary land, and they came here to find things they could not find at home. Once here, they had to invent their lives. It was not simply a matter of choosing among the many possibilities. It was also inventing possibilities that were not yet seen. The idea of the inventor, from Benjamin Franklin to Steve Jobs, was a metaphor for what American life consisted of. The invented people invented things and invented themselves. And for this to happen, the American had to discover his own self-reliance and add that to the courage he had displayed simply

GEORGE FRIEDMAN

in coming here. There were many vices attached to Americans, as there are to all people, but these were the virtues, a combination that created a unique people.

It is impossible to fully describe a people, but it is even harder to describe a people who didn't exist until a few centuries ago. Americans are a people whose existence unfolded over that time, both from immigration and from transformation. Immigrants changed the dynamic of the American people, but it was the constant transformation of everyday life, by shifting geography, technology, and wars, that constantly changed what it meant to be an American. There was one thing that all Americans had in common: they left the things they were born to, and they desired to come to America. In each generation more came, and in each generation the memory of who their family once was grew dim, yet rarely faded into nothingness. Those whose roots were in England or who came from Ireland or Poland knew that in some way those roots still held them in their grip. Even those who came from Africa remembered who they once were. Perhaps because they came against their will to live in misery, they clung to their past more than others.

This duality is the essential nature of the United States from the English settlers onward. Their past was with their family lineage. Their future with the United States. And over time the familial and the national blurred into each other. All of this was rooted in geopolitics. The English population that had first occupied the Eastern Seaboard was insufficient to control the continent. Even including African American slaves, there was simply not enough population. The Constitution, Article 1, Section 8, had recognized this, stating the method by which immigrants might be naturalized. The founders had understood this problem and prepared the regime for it. The first wave of migrants was Scots-Irish, Scottish Presbyterians who had settled in Ireland. Their hunger was for land and freedom from elites. They were a rowdy bunch, seen by many of those of English heritage as unassimilable. They were not the last to be labeled as such.

The first core culture of the United States was the culture of the first English settler. Initially, this meant English and Protestant. The white Anglo-Saxon Protestant remained the defining center of American culture until after World War II, when the vast numbers of other nationalities and religions were integrated into the military, side by side with the WASPs. With that, the idea that the WASPs were the American culture declined, save for one thing: the English language, which was always at the center of the American experience. One could choose not to learn English but would then be excluded from the economic and social life of America. Because immigrants came here precisely for the social and economic benefits, refusing to learn English was self-defeating.

There are three symbols that give us a sense of the American. One is the cowboy and his complex relationship to duty, evil, and women. The second is the inventor, who both imagines and creates the extraordinary things that compel America forward. Finally, there is the warrior. The United States is a paradox. Dedicated to the pursuit of happiness, America was born in battle and has fought many wars since. The warrior lives by duty, not happiness, yet is integral to American culture. The cowboy, the inventor, and the warrior all speak to the dynamic that forces the United States into storms from which progress emerges.

There is of course one thing beyond these stereotypes. When I think of an American, I think of subtlety. I'm aware that subtlety is not normally associated with being American. Americans are regarded as unsophisticated and uncultured. There may be truth to that, but the ability to come to a strange land and make a living, the ability to live with constantly changing technology and customs, the ability to remain oriented in land constantly being redefined, requires a great deal of subtlety and depth. This is where American resilience comes from, and nowhere is resilience more recognizable than in the myth of the cowboy.

The Cowboy

Let's begin with the quintessential American image: the cowboy, presented in the quintessential American art form, the movies. The cowboy is what Europeans accuse Americans of being and what defines manliness to both American men and women. A cowboy is strong, laconic, fearless, and with an unshakable will to do what is right. His virtue is not in his depth but in his actions.

The reality of the cowboys was different from the movie portrayal. They were significant for only about twenty years, until railroads expanded. Many were African American, Mexican, and Indian, joined by poor whites, many of them recent immigrants. The movies portrayed them as white, with perhaps a Mexican cook. And most movies portrayed gunmen and lawmen, without a cow in sight. Most of these movies were simply entertainment. But the best of them portrayed a deeper subtlety about the mythical cowboy, in which what he appears to be and what his life is all about are profoundly different.

The movie *High Noon,* considered one of the finest of the genre, shows the surprising subtlety of the gunfighter's life. Gary Cooper plays Will Kane, a lawman in a New Mexico town who has just married Amy, played by Grace Kelly. They are about to leave on their honeymoon. But before they can leave town, a band of four outlaws shows up intending to kill Kane.

Amy had become a pacifist and Quaker after her father and brother were gunned down. She wants Kane to flee with her to avoid a fight and likely death. Kane is torn between his new bride's wishes and protecting his town against the outlaws. We discover, however, that it is more than wife versus town. The struggle is between two strands of the American character. One is the ideal of manly courage confronting the lurking evil. The other is the dissenter tradition of English Protestantism. The man embodies the tradition of courage. The woman embodies the tradition of Christian gentleness.

Kane sees himself as doing his duty as a lawman defending the town. But he discovers that the town he polices doesn't support him. Some people are afraid; some sympathize with the outlaws; some hold grudges against Kane. There are endless reasons for them not to support Kane in the upcoming fight against the outlaws. Kane is, therefore, alone against evil.

Kane is not serving the town but doing his duty to himself. In the song accompanying the movie, there is a warning about going to the grave as a "craven coward." For Kane, this isn't really about the town or his oath as town marshal. It is about his duty to himself. Instead of leaving on his honeymoon, he puts on his badge and gun belt. He will be a man even to the grave. And when he does so, a gulf opens between him and his wife, between the warrior tradition and Christianity.

But the story takes a twist. The four outlaws come at Kane in a swirling gunfight. Kane kills two, and when another waits in ambush for him, Kane's wife takes a shotgun and shoots the gunman in the back. She couldn't abandon her husband, and saves him by abandoning her moral principles and ruthlessly killing a man. Then, when the last desperado is facing Kane, he grabs Amy, holding her hostage, and orders Kane to drop his gun. Kane is about to do that when Amy reaches up and rakes the desperado's eyes. She breaks free from him, and Kane shoots him down. Kane then embraces his wife, drops his badge in the dirt, and leaves with her.

High Noon portrays Kane as calm, determined, and unemotional. But it isn't Kane who is the hero of the movie. It is his wife. She abandons her religious beliefs and her oath to herself in order to save her husband's life. Unlike Kane, who would not shoot a man in the back without warning, Amy has no such compunctions. Nor will she refrain from what a man might call "fighting dirty" when she scratches the eyes of the last gunman standing, giving Kane an open shot. Her duty is to what she loves, and everything else is secondary. Had Kane's wife stood her moral ground the way her husband had, Kane would be dead. He couldn't give. She could. Her love for him transcended her religion, transcended the rules of war. Kane was forced into action by his fear of being a coward. Amy decided the future. Kane is simplistic in his morality. Amy bears the complexity of Christianity in a New England town, where she had been born. It is the woman, not the man, who bears the burden of moral ambiguity, and her willingness to do so saves Kane from himself.

The movie also displays the sense of dread that haunts the American character. The gunmen that have come to kill Kane are menacing and self-confident. They lack any human emotion beyond menace. Their goal is to kill, and they know that they will succeed. We know from one of them that he had been sent to prison and then, for some nameless and unnerving reason, was pardoned. Who these men were, where they came from, and what their end goal was beyond killing Kane is unknown. There is no sign of family, pity, fear, or anything connecting them to anyone but each other, and the only thing that connects them is a will to do evil. They are a frightening force coming into a small town from out of an endless prairie.

Like most small towns of the day, this town is isolated, connected to the world only by an intermittent train. The inhabitants don't know what is lurking out on the prairie. All they know is that they are alone in the vastness, and it is a frightening thought. But it is no different being in a large city. The aloneness of a city filled with people is real and the sense of isolation powerful. The fear of danger from evil is as real in a city as it is in a small town out west.

There is a rootlessness in America that is part of its strength. People move about freely without the constraint of family and tradition. The people who moved to Kane's town did not have generations of community to draw on any more than a new arrival to Chicago did. The rootlessness of America is simultaneously liberating and frightening, containing the fear of an unknown evil lurking in the darkness. The police are far away, and the neighbors are as afraid as you are.

The subtlety of *High Noon* is that it allows the viewer to see the western lawman as a cliché. He is a hard man, unbending in his view of what is right, fearless of even insurmountable odds. He would also be dead if that were the end of the story. Frequently unrecognized, Kane's wife is the decisive character, acting in opposition to her moral values. Morality starts as a simple concept and becomes complicated. The relationship between a man and a woman starts as a simple concept. It becomes enormously complex.

The movie, a Western no less, points toward the complex evolution taking place in American society. *High Noon* was filmed in 1952, seven years after World War II ended. World War II called for men to be like Kane, more afraid of cowardice than of death. *High Noon* was about the West, but it was also about World War II and the way men had to behave if they weren't to go mad. The men fought the war, but the women won it.

Women won the war in a very traditional sense. Men go to war for their beliefs, for their country, and for their families. There is an ancient dynamic in war, and many stereotypes associated with it. In the minds of men, women will forgive anything but weakness. War is the ultimate test of strength, and soldiers offer it to women as proof of strength. Women comfort men when they come home from war temporarily weakened and make them strong again. These are typecasts but also ancient truths, and there was an empathy between men and women that makes the pain of war bearable.

Women also won World War II in a radically new way. It was an industrial war. U.S. success had to do with production. Sixty-five percent of the U.S. aircraft industry workers were women. Twenty-five percent of married women worked outside the home, and 37 percent of the total workforce during the war was composed of women. In all 350,000 women served in the armed forces. The pilots who flew the bombers from the factory to the combat airfield were women. The United States could not have defeated the Germans and Japanese without women. The Soviet Union and Britain were able to resist and destroy the Germans only because of the equipment the United States gave them. It was the Soviet army that broke the back of the Wehrmacht and made the conquest of France possible. They broke the back of the Wehrmacht only because of the equipment produced by American women.

The core of all cultures is the relationship between men and women. For most of human history, the relationship was defined and constrained by biological and demographic reality. For the population to be stable, women needed to give birth to as many children as they could before they died, often in childbirth. Men labored and often had multiple wives in parallel or in sequence. Marriage was about social and personal necessity. Women were essential, and yet the key role they played in human reproduction put them at severe risk. The evolution of modern medicine and sanitation changed all this. Women lived much longer, perhaps eighty years instead of forty, having one or two children instead of eight, and therefore a productive life outside the household became possible.

In 1963, Betty Friedan published *The Feminine Mystique,* which many regard as the beginning of contemporary feminism. By the end of the century, the role of women had transformed in the United States. It had also created a dimension of our cyclical process that will have to be understood. Feminism has many dimensions. Intellectually, it formally recognized the transforming biological reality of women's lives and the radical possibilities opened up by this transformation. It included the end to the compulsory distinctions between men and women and the transformation of the relationship between them. We have gone from an inescapable and desperate struggle to reproduce . . . to marriage as the result of romantic affinity and free choice . . . to the virtual collapse of the courtship ritual.

The deeper point is the speed at which ancient norms changed in the United States. We speak of social and economic mobility. But at the root of America is cultural mobility. There are many startling things about American life, but none more startling than the unprecedented speed with which the role of women changed and the speed at which sexual relationships shifted. The shift has created a great uncertainty.

However courageous Kane's wife is in *High Noon,* after it is all over, she will go home with Kane and have his children. Her underlying Christianity would be shocked by what life has become a hundred years later. The unification of sex and reproduction within marriage used to define the role of women. Grace Kelly as Amy in *High Noon* and Rosie the Riveter unintentionally revealed that the role of women as traditionally performed and viewed as a moral necessity suddenly became one of many options available as part of the pursuit of happiness.

The Inventor

High Noon was a movie, and movies could not have been made without movie cameras. The man who invented the movie camera was Thomas Edison. Edison had made his fortune inventing applications for electricity. He did not discover electricity, nor was he the first to understand its importance. Benjamin Franklin had plumbed its complexity. What Edison did do was to create an organization designed to find applications for electricity, and to create a business to turn those applications into wealth, sometimes by building and selling the product, but far more often by selling the applications to other businesses that took on the task of marketing and selling the product.

The world had been filled with other inventors, such as Nikola Tesla, who had done a great deal of work in the area of electricity but had never created a truly successful business. What Edison did was to combine the art of invention with an understanding of business. Edison grasped what others had missed. Technology is intended to create products, and products must be sold. He understood the subtlety of invention, which was not mastering the science nor building the product. The subtlety was in understanding what society needed and what the customer would buy. It was not enough to be a scientist or an engineer. It was also necessary to be a sociologist. Thomas Edison became the template for Henry Ford, Bill Gates, Elon Musk, and all of the rest who understood that the inventor had to have a user and that business was the bridge between the two.

Edison was born in Ohio and grew up in Michigan. He was schooled at home by his mother. Aside from an interest in books on nature, there was nothing in his childhood to predict what he would achieve. There is a saying attributed to him that helps explain his thinking: "Opportunity is missed by most people because it is dressed in overalls and looks like work." Another is, "Genius is one part inspiration and ninety-nine parts perspiration." What he said was simple. Yet the insight is far from obvious.

Edison's most important contribution was a structure for inventing things. He created the first industrial research laboratory in Menlo Park, New Jersey, by designing a method for invention that used teams. He also developed a principle for inventing things, saying that inventions should be driven by what the market required. He became the first marketer of technology, turning his name into a household word and turning himself into a celebrity. He turned inventiveness into a multi-team effort, managed by him and driven by market opportunities, and he built the marketing effort around his personality.

When we think about other technologists selling consumer products, from Henry Ford (a close friend of Edison's) to Steve Jobs, we see the model that has emerged. The lonely inventor is replaced by the team. The goal is not to make basic scientific discoveries but to apply science to products. The effort was closely related to the market, and the broader the market, the better. One dreamed of turning the night into day, another of making transportation affordable, and the last of making the computer a household appliance with endless applications. For all three, the purpose was to make enormous amounts of money, but at the same time there was an unintended political end, which was to enhance democratic life by increasing happiness. And these men shared the profound idea that a movie camera, an automobile, and a computer would do both. As technology changes, so does the business model, but the core, the idea of business, remains a constant, and the inventor as businessperson remains essential to American life.

Business existed as the counterbalance to the state. The founders mistrusted the state, but it was the repository of military power. The corporate world, itself fragmented, was the repository of wealth. Each blocked the other's ability to rule absolutely, and both cooperated in pursuing mutual interests. The founders understood that the private sphere without power could never control the state, however divided. But the founders were also private men of affairs, men of business. And they knew that the existence of business interests both corrupted and undermined the state, while at the same time the state could cripple business.

In the creation of the Great Seal, an unspoken deal was struck, which has been there since the founding: the deal between political and economic power. It is a deal that has been condemned from the beginning of the Republic, but it is a deal that will never go away. After all, someone had to have the contract for the pyramid the founders wanted built. From the beginning, the United States was the confrontation and cooperation of money and politics, and of the application of both to war.

The Warrior

America is a warrior culture. That would seem to be contrary to the discussion of Thomas Edison, not because he was a pacifist, but because he was a technologist and a businessman. Technology and business are dedicated to pleasing customers and making money, to pursuing happiness. War is about sacrifice and duty. I can say that America is about business. I can also say that America is about making war. The contradiction is real, and it is hard to reconcile. Yet in speaking of the subtlety of the American people, I will argue the two have lived side by side from the beginning.

As I have said, the United States was born in battle, eight brutal years of unrelenting warfare in which twenty-five thousand American soldiers died. Because there were about 2.5 million Americans alive during the war, this meant that 1 percent of the population died, a higher percentage than in any other war. Virtually every generation had its wars. Many were small with few warriors, and some wars were enormous.

Consider this number. There are approximately twenty-five million men and women either serving in the U.S. armed forces or veterans of them alive at this moment. That is a staggering number, but it does not capture the whole picture. A soldier is not alone in war. There are parents, spouses, children, and other relatives who all experience war through the soldiers, sometimes while they serve and sometimes afterward, through their memories. They are affected by war almost as deeply as the warriors. Assuming that there are on average four people whose lives are shaped or reshaped by someone's service, that means that about a hundred million Americans have had their lives shaped by war or the possibility of war. That is almost one-third of the country.

Thirty years after the revolution, the United States fought the War of 1812. About thirty-four years later, there was the war with Mexico, and then about thirteen years after that the Civil War broke out. Six hundred thousand Americans died. After this, there was the long final struggle with the Indian nations. Then there was the Spanish-American War in 1898. Sixteen years after that was World War I, and twenty-three years after that World War II. Then came Korea and Vietnam and, since the beginning of the twenty-first century, the wars against the jihadists.

As we will see, there are geopolitical reasons for the increasing frequency of war. But the cultural question is more puzzling. How does the culture of war coexist with the culture of happiness? A simple answer is that warriors have always occupied a unique place in societies. Placing oneself between one's beloved home and war's desolation has been seen as the noblest of things. War has traditionally been a test of manhood, of courage, duty, and strength.

The attraction of war may be as simple as that. The United States is a nation, all nations fight wars, and the warrior occupies a special place that men—and now women—crave. But the United States differs from other nations in that it has another class of heroes: those who raise themselves from nothing to great wealth. Both fight battles, and both can claim to fight for themselves and for their country. In America some people can do both, and they are admired most of all.

But there is a deeper synergy. I've been talking about progress, technology, and business. We need to take this process apart a bit to understand how it all fits together and understand the cultural alignment and tension that arise. There are three parts. The first is basic science, the understanding of the underlying reality of nature.

The second is technology, the transformation of basic science into tools for using nature. The third is the product, something that can be used to achieve certain ends.

The battle of *High Noon* was fought in New Mexico, which was also the home of the greatest scientific battle, the development of the atomic bomb. The lonely deserts and towns of New Mexico were the places where the atomic bomb was designed, assembled, and tested. It was the place where the university met the military. The scientists, like Kane, gave everything to confront and destroy the evil that was stalking the earth. Ever since the Manhattan Project built the bomb in New Mexico, the military has been obsessed with basic science and with the scientist. In their work, scientists laid the ground for defeating the enemy and building American power beyond what was dreamed. New Mexico was a vast and empty space, in the part of the American West where wood, water, and people were hard to come by. It was a place where things could be hidden out in the open.

The atomic bomb posed a moral dilemma. As with Grace Kelly's character in *High Noon,* the Americans chose victory and survival over the moral absolute. America was designed by the founders as a moral undertaking. As such it was offended by what was necessary to the nation. The argument began at the founding. It was decided in the desolate places of America, where few lived.

Whether the Colt .45 or the bomb called Little Boy, the morality and the weaponry are joined together in American culture. After World War II, the intimate connection between war as a moral project and technology intersected to create a new foundation of American society. For example, the Department of Defense needed a very lightweight computer for its Minuteman missile's guidance system. DOD approached civilian scientists and engineers to create it. In 1956 Jack Kilby, who worked for Texas Instruments, invented the integrated circuit, the microchip. It was installed in the Minuteman missile in 1962. The prototype of a microchip-based computer was created to guide ICBMs. By the 1970s, it was being integrated into systems created by Steve Jobs and Bill Gates to create the home computer.

The NAVSTAR system was introduced by the Department of Defense in 1973. Its purpose was to provide precision navigation for the American military. The method used by NAVSTAR was developed by physicists studying Einstein's theory of relativity. The Department of Defense built a constellation of satellites around the physicists' work that made precision navigation and guidance for weapons possible. Its popular name became GPS, and it became a commonplace part of everyday life.

During the 1960s, U.S. secret research facilities needed a secure method for rapidly sharing data. The Advanced Research Projects Agency of the Department of Defense was the first to apply the well-known theory of the movement of data over phone lines. The system developed from this application was called ARPANET, and it evolved into today's Internet. The degree to which the Defense Department reshaped everyday life is rarely fully appreciated.

The Manhattan Project transformed the American character in this way. There had always been a struggle between morality and violence. The atomic bomb simply extended the issue to more extreme levels. But the core tension between courage, the weapon, justice, and morality remained the same as it did before. What changed was the dramatically greater capabilities of the weapons and the manner in which the technology transformed society as a whole. The distinction between peace and war, between the warrior, the civilian, the scientist, and the businessman became increasingly difficult to see. Edison's pride in never having produced a weapon was not really true at the time and has become impossible today.

There is technology, there is business, and there is war. They appear to be different, but in American life the scientist, cowboy, and warrior, and add to this the businessman, are part of a single culture. The culture is one of contradiction but also reconciliation.

GEORGE FRIEDMAN

These are profoundly different types of people, and it would be assumed that they would have little to do with each other. And on a personal level that might be true. But they form a single fabric of American society. Myriad others are not mentioned here, but these three give a sense of the complexity and subtlety of America. It makes it a hard place to live and a tense one. It is not easy to be American. Europeans see the cowboy as simplistic. Americans live lives of complexity and friction.

It is the contradictions within the American people that drive the rapidly evolving cycles of their history. The unity of the utterly diverse—the cowboy, the scientist, the inventor-businessman, the warrior—constantly reinvents America in an endless cycle of rise and fall. It is the tension between types of Americans (and I have pointed out only a fraction) that makes it impossible to pin down the American character. That character is built of contradictions far greater than exist in nations that didn't invent themselves as recently and aren't still in the process of reinventing themselves. Europeans and Asians have millennia of history and culture to look back on. Americans have only the future to consider, and the future must be invented over and over again. The regime was invented. The use of the continent was invented, and the nation was invented. And that invention both continues and creates the constant pressure to abandon what Americans were, in favor of what they will become. It is a lonely undertaking as each generation abandons its past, and this process creates the restless cycles of American life and the resilience to recover from the inevitable storms.

Crimes of the Nation: Slavery and Indians

No discussion of the invention of the United States is permissible without addressing the glaring moral crimes of the nation. There is a saying attributed to Balzac that behind every great fortune there is a great crime, and in the case of the great American fortune there are two to consider. One is the enslavement of Africans, and the other is genocide against Indians. These two charges are regarded by some as undermining any claim to moral authority that the United States might have. Given that the United States is, as I have said, a moral project, the charges have to be taken with utmost seriousness and cannot be minimized. The United States bears enormous national guilt for both transgressions, but as with most matters, moral and historical, the story is more complex than the way it is normally addressed, and therefore incomplete. The guilt is real. At the same time there is an explanation, though certainly not a justification.

Slavery was introduced to the Western Hemisphere centuries before there was a United States or even a settlement of North America. The Portuguese and the Spanish both enslaved American Indians, and the Portuguese transported Africans to Brazil. Brazil by far held the most Africans in bondage. The Spanish, the Dutch, and the English introduced slavery into North America in the early seventeenth century, at a time when there were no Americans, just European settlers.

In this sense, slavery was a shared crime, but the United States did something that I would regard as monstrous. The United States not only carried on the practice of slavery but defined Africans formally and legally as subhuman. The Declaration of Independence held that all men are created equal. The founders believed this yet wanted to continue the practice of African enslavement. They knew they could not create the United States without allowing slavery to continue in the South, because the South would not have joined the Union. The founders therefore solved the problem with what can only be considered a moral crime. Because all men were created equal, Africans were declared less than human, and the Constitution institutionalized their moral worth at three-fifths of a white's.

This was an unforgivable sin of the United States. Men like Jefferson and Adams certainly knew African Americans were equal,

71

but for economic and political convenience they consented to accept the doctrine that they were not.

The Declaration of Independence was meant to be a beacon to the world. Slavery preceded the discovery of the United States, and was practiced widely and continued to be practiced elsewhere even after 1865, but by perverting the founding document of the nation, the founding fathers created lasting injustice toward African Americans. The document enshrined the sub-humanity of African Americans in American culture in a way that demeaned its victims and created a viciousness that still corrupts the nation and continues to stigmatize the victims that were intended to be set free. Law shapes culture, and the abolition of a law does not by itself change the culture.

The second crime with which the United States must contend is genocide against the Indians. This is a complex matter. Recent studies of the decimation of the natives of the Western Hemisphere make it clear that it was disease, not acts of violence, that killed not only North American Indians but Indians throughout the hemisphere. Measles, smallpox, and other diseases wiped out as much as 90 percent of some Indian nations. The Europeans brought with them diseases they were unaware of. Having no theory of the origin of disease, they decimated a population that had no natural defenses against them. The book *1491* by Charles C. Mann describes the process of depopulation in detail.

Many of the Indian nations encountered by Americans as they moved westward were the shattered and fragmented remains of what had once been great nations. The Americans drew a judgment of the Indian based on these remnants. But not all the Indian nations were fragmented. One in particular, the Comanche, had established a vast empire ranging from the Rockies to Texas and Kansas. From the eighteenth century onward, they had terrorized other Indian nations, particularly the Plains Indians. These nations and tribes where therefore savaged in three ways. One was by disease introduced by the Europeans. The second was by the Comanche empire, which also terrorized European settlers. And the third was by the Europeans, who took advantage of the destabilization of the Plains Indians in order to kill the remnants or herd them into places reserved for them, like parts of Oklahoma.

The story of the destruction of the Indian nations has much to do with the formation of the United States, but it is far more complex than simply the actions of the United States. It is not clear that absent disease and Comanche warfare, the Americans could have settled the West. There had been many more Indians before the plagues, and they were both sophisticated and warlike. The settlers had the guns, but the arrows were not trivial.

Above all it should be remembered that each Indian nation and tribe saw the others as foreign. They saw themselves not as one continental people but as separate nations with separate languages and beliefs. Like nations everywhere in the world, they constantly made war and alliances with each other. In many cases, the Indian nations saw the advancing Americans as allies against historic enemies. During the American advance in the West, the Americans found not only nations decimated by disease or crushed by the Comanche but also allies pleased to see the Americans arrive and join them in war against their enemies. In a certain sense, they saw the Americans as simply another alien tribe. Therefore the moral standard that must be used in evaluating the Americans is the degree to which they imposed destruction on the Indians and the degree to which disease and Indian collaboration were involved. As in the history of any continent, the history of warfare in North America is far more ancient and complex than simply one nation being at fault for all others. If there was a moral crime, it was far more complex than it is frequently treated.

But diseases had dramatically reduced the Indian populations, and those who were confronted by the United States were frequently so frightened of other tribes that they made alliances first with

Europeans and then with Americans. Americans took advantage of all of this, killing more Indians, conquering their lands, and then signing treaties with sovereign Indian nations just as they would have with other nations. But the United States violated almost all of those treaties. This was an integral part of the crime. Americans were not responsible for the complex politics and warfare waged by Indian nations against other Indian nations. Nor were Americans responsible for the disease they brought. But they were guilty of confronting Indian nations and waging war and then systematically betraying them in every way possible in making peace. In so doing, the United States turned a bearable defeat into total dispossession of an Indian population.

PART TWO

AMERICAN CYCLES

4

How America Changes

The title of this book is *The Storm Before the Calm*. It is in general about the United States, but in particular about the idiosyncratic way the country evolves. The United States periodically reaches a point of crisis in which it appears to be at war with itself, yet after an extended period it reinvents itself, in a form both faithful to its founding and radically different from what it had been. In part 1, I explained the United States as an invented nation, with the regime, the people, and even the land constantly being re-created. That created periods of deep tension. In this section, I want to talk about the cycles of crises, order, and reinvention that have shaped the country and will portend events into the 2020s and beyond.

We tend to evaluate America based on day-to-day news stories and immediate trends and feelings, but the larger wheels of America are driven by two very orderly cycles—the institutional and the socioeconomic. The institutional cycle controls the relationship between the federal government and the rest of American society, and it runs its course roughly every eighty years. The socioeconomic cycle shifts about every fifty years and alters the dynamic of the American economy and society. Each cycle goes through the same process. The characteristics of a current cycle stop being effective, and the model begins to break down. A period of political tension emerges, ultimately forcing a change in the way things are done. New models emerge and solve the problems, and the country begins a new cycle which operates until that cycle runs into trouble. Why it takes eighty and fifty years, respectively, will be explained along with their other complexities.

This is how the United States was designed to evolve. Over the course of nearly 250 years, it has changed dramatically, from a third world country clinging to the edge of the Atlantic to the dominant global power. What is perhaps most remarkable is that the United States did not tear itself apart due to the speed and pressures of change. Even the Civil War ultimately set the stage for peaceful and dramatic national development. The basic questions that have to be answered are why the United States evolved as dramatically as it did, why it didn't tear itself apart, and where it goes from here.

Invention aside, it should not really surprise us that a nation of over 300 million people will generate orderly and predictable cycles. Human existence consists of cycles. We are born, we are nurtured, we have a childhood, an adulthood, and then old age and death. All of nature is built on cycles, and therefore it would be very odd if human society did not also develop cyclically. The human cycles are different depending on where those humans are located, who their neighbors are, and how their nations came to be. In different places, cycles are much longer or much shorter or more, or less, predictable. The American cycle matches the American nature. Stemming from the first immigrants' sense of urgency to earn a living, Americans are impatient by nature, and that impatience leads to action, and that action leads to cycles that are both orderly and, by the measure of history, rapid.

We tend to think of our lives as matters of choice. But that isn't true. There are exceptions to the rule, and certainly there are outliers, but generally speaking if you were born in Burundi, you will have a different life from someone born in Kansas. Where we are born, who our parents were, and what resources they had, how smart and talented we are, and all the other variables constrain what we can do. We all live in a world of constraints, where many things are simply impossible to us. We make choices, but those choices exist within narrow boundaries. As we grow older, the tighter the constraints get. It is those constraints that permit us to predict the approximate course of a life. There is obviously a level in which humans make their own choices, but as Adam Smith pointed out, all those individual choices lead to a predictable nation. It is predictability that is behind the orderliness of American cycles.

Political leaders spend years seeking power. The struggle to reach the top makes them painfully aware of the forces that they must master. Those forces continue to shape their actions while they're at the top. Those who reach the pinnacle of leadership endured a grueling struggle. Americans tend to think leaders, particularly those they don't like, got there by bad luck. There is always far more to it than that.

The American president's agenda is set not by his intentions but by the limits of his powers and the pressure placed on him by the social and economic conditions at home and the competing interests of foreign powers. He can ignore none of these. Presidents know, or learn very quickly, that the constraints on their activities define what their presidency will be like. George W. Bush did not come to office imagining he would be defined by 9/11 and its aftermath. Barack Obama came to office convinced that he could change the American relationship with the Islamic world. Trump came into office thinking he would rebuild American industry. For all of them, what remained of their illusions of power was quickly dissipated. Political power is not about whim. It is about understanding realities.

Arguing that a president is a product of events and not their creator goes against the intense passions we feel for, or against, particular presidents. But the idea that impersonal forces govern us, and that we prosper to the extent we conform to those forces, is an everyday idea. It is how we think of the marketplace. We understand that it consists of billions of decisions made by millions of people and that the behavior of all these people, taken as a whole, can be to a significant degree predicted. The president cannot simply intervene and will the market to behave in a different way and end recessions. To the extent he or the Fed can do anything, it comes from recognizing what the problem is and what the solution is.

If there is regularity to history, and if presidents survive only to the extent that they recognize and conform to those constraints, then it is possible to benchmark where we are and to forecast where we are going. It is possible to locate where America is in its cycle. Knowing roughly when the crisis posed by the unsolved problem reaches the breaking point, we can predict two things. First, we can predict how the problem will be solved, by identifying the unique solution required. And then we can forecast when the political system will spasm, generating a president who rejects the old cycle and begins groping for ways to implement the solution. He does not make history. History makes him.

There is also a deeper global current that affects how nations operate and establishes the hierarchy of dominance. After the collapse of the Soviet Union, that current shifted away from Europe to the United States as the center of gravity of the world. The fact that the United States sits in this position means that its institutional, economic, cultural, and technical forces have profound effects on the rest of the globe. Consider the impact of the microchip or an American recession on companies, jobs, and people's lives worldwide. In the same sense that Britain and Rome defined their worlds at the height of their powers, so will the United States. The internal pressures of the American cycles will inevitably translate into global pressures elsewhere. It is these internal cycles, combined with global currents, that have created a uniquely uncomfortable moment for the United States.

5

How Geopolitics
Frames the 2020s

In the introduction, I spoke of the crisis of the 2020s, the period in which the two major cycles will combine to destabilize the nation and set the stage for the new phase in American life. The crisis of the 2020s will be abnormal not only because the two crises will combine into one but because the United States has reached an unprecedented point in its history. It has become the preeminent power in the world, and it doesn't know if it wants the honor or how to manage it. This frames and intensifies the coming crisis of the 2020s.

The two major cyclical forces will shift during the 2020s, the first time that both have done so in the same decade. This will compound instability. But another force will compound it further. The United States was founded as a marginal country, clinging to the East Coast, threatened by larger powers. It has grown from this into the preeminent global power. This has placed stresses on the United States that increase institutional, economic, and social processes. This new status has been accompanied by over eighteen years of combat in the Middle East, the threat of terrorism, and global interests and ensuing frictions. During the 2020s, the stress on the Republic caused by the new geopolitical reality will intensify the pressures on the United States.

Institutional cycles have historically been driven by war: the Revolutionary War, the Civil War, and World War II. The next institutional cycle is also emerging from war. On the surface, this is the war the United States has fought against jihadists since 2001. But there is a deeper shift that has generated this war. It is the radical shift in the American position in the global system. That shift helped generate Islamist hostility toward the United States after Operation Desert Storm. Desert Storm was triggered not only by the Iraqi invasion of Kuwait but by the fact that the United States, now the sole global power, had to create and lead a coalition to fight the war. The international conflict framing the new institutional cycle isn't nearly as bloody as the others, but it is perhaps even more profound.

In 1991 the Soviet Union collapsed, and for the first time in five hundred years no European country was a global power. The end of this five-hundred-year-long geopolitical cycle left the United States as the world's dominant and only global power. That not only changed the position of the United States but challenged its institutional, social, and economic configuration. America's political system had never anticipated this role on this scale and did not know how to structure the machinery of the United States to cope with it. So the crisis of the 2020s–2030s is indeed part of a continuous process of cycles that dominate American history. But it is also taking place in an utterly new context, one that increases the tensions inherent in the American historical process.

The United States has become an empire. It is an empire of power and global reach, but of course not a formal empire. Its power derives from the size of its economy, its military, and the seductive power of its culture. These in turn derive from its regime, land, and people. It is all the more impressive because it has no formal structure. It simply is the most powerful agent, for good or bad, in the world. It is also a nation that is profoundly uncomfortable being an empire. The United States, in 1776, had the first modern uprising against an existing empire, and as a nation it does not welcome the dangers and complexities of global responsibility. It did not become an empire by choice, nor can it abandon the reality of what it is. The United States is a young country and an even younger empire. Its vast power maintains it even in the face of its ineptness or global condemnation. The United States is learning how to be an empire, creating enormous pressures on the world and on American institutions and the American public. Nowhere is this more obvious than in the clumsy management of the eighteen-year war against the jihadists.

An empire exists when its power is so great compared with other nations that simply by existing, it changes the shape of their relationships and the way other nations behave. There are empires built out of intention, such as Hitler's. There are empires that emerge without any intention. Rome didn't intend to be an empire. The inability of Europe to contain its violent tendencies caused it to lose its own formal empires while leaving a vacuum that the United States and the Soviet Union were drawn into. With the collapse of the Soviet Union, there remained regional powers, but no global ones except for the United States.

America existed as a nation in a particular place and with a particular people, but unlike most other nations it was founded as a moral project, a place where both human rights and the national interest could thrive. The United States has been torn since its founding between these two principles. Today, with the vast power of the United States and its global impact, this distinction has intensified the conflict between values: morality and nation. Alongside this tension is another. There are those who want to emulate what they think the founders wished, which was to avoid foreign entanglements. There are others who argue that only a deep and continual involvement in the world can satisfy American needs. These two arguments are linked, and have been going on in the United States since its founding, but inevitably are getting more intense today. At every NATO meeting, at every discussion with China, this tension arises.

On one side is the argument that the primary mission of the United States is to be an exemplar of moral virtue and that American power should be used to protect and spread American principles. At the root of this position is the view that the United States has an obligation to itself and the world to advocate and defend the moral principles on which it was founded, and the belief that behaving like any other country and defending its economic and strategic interests betrays America's mission. The problem with this view is that most nations don't adhere to American moral standards and U.S. power is greatly limited. This is a formula for endless war.

On the other side are those who make the argument that the primary interest of the United States is to protect America, its land and its people. To do that, it must engage in the world like any other nation. Principles cannot survive without power. This argument believes that American values cannot survive if the United States doesn't survive, and those interests can best be spread through American power. That means that the United States must at times take actions that would seem to run counter to American principles, but weakening or losing the United States serves no principles. Spreading American values sometimes requires abandoning them. In World War II, the United States allied with Joseph Stalin's Soviet Union. This was both essential and horrifying.

This is not an argument between ideologies. Today, elements of both the Left and the Right make the case for spreading American values. On the Left, human rights advocates argue that the United States must use its power and influence to punish regimes that violate human rights, understood as the liberal democratic principles on which the United States was founded. On the Right, neoconservatives argue that the United States ought to use its power to help shape the world according to American principles. Both are prepared to use military power, economic pressure, or funding political groups to pursue their ends. The neoconservatives explicitly argue that U.S. power and force are needed for moral ends. The Left is more limited in the advocacy of the use of force, but advocated it in cases like Rwanda and Libya, where the state was harming its own people. The Left and the Right think of themselves as opposed to each other, but nuances aside, they follow the idea that the purpose of U.S. power is to project American principles.

This argument has raged since the nation's founding. The French Revolution occurred shortly after the founding of the United States and emulated most American principles. At the same time, the United States was dependent on England for trade, and England was hostile to the French Revolution. On the one side was moral principle. On the other side was the national interest. Washington chose national interest, and Jefferson, the man of principle, did not argue.

The debate between morality and national security touches on a second debate, somewhat different from the first. This is the debate between avoiding foreign entanglements and pursuing the national interest through constant involvement in the world. Although this entanglement has never stopped, many today still speak fondly of a time, before they were born, in which the United States looked out for itself. It neither asked for help nor gave it, separated from the world by two massive oceans.

In fact, such a time never existed. The United States was born out of a European war, the struggle between England and France. Had these two global powers not been battling each other, the United States would not have come into existence. The United States was far too weak and disorganized to defeat England, except that the English army and navy were forced to divert their attention from insurrection in the North American colonies to deal with a much more pressing enemy, France. The founders knew they couldn't win without taking advantage of that war. They sent Benjamin Franklin to Paris to represent the colonies and to seek an intervention by the

French in North America. France had its hands full with England and could provide minimal help, sending military advisers like Lafayette to help organize the American military.

The French promised much but could deliver little. The founders, sophisticated in foreign affairs, played the French along, while the French played the colonists along. The French made promises in order to maintain the Americans' confidence and keep them fighting and pinning down some English troops. The Americans, Franklin in particular, knew the French couldn't divert their forces to help the United States but kept his colleagues in America committed to a French strategy, and the French committed to an American strategy. In the end, the French freed enough naval forces to allow Washington to defeat Cornwallis and the British at Yorktown, at the same time that a French fleet bombarded them. From the beginning of its existence, the United States was engaged in diplomacy, power politics, wars, and every foreign entanglement imaginable. That was inevitable. Nations rarely last long if they aren't aware of foreign threats and opportunities. Nevertheless, in spite of the reality, there is a longing in American culture for a time that never was.

The debate over power politics and American ideas, and between American isolation and involvement in the world, defined American foreign policy historically. It was a recurrent theme with generally one set of answers. At the same time, the answer made the United States uneasy. That uneasiness was present at the transition of the United States from one nation among many to the preeminent power in the world, an empire. Part of that tradition involved a fundamental change in how the United States viewed the world.

Pearl Harbor changed everything. The United States was expecting war with Japan, but it was vastly confident that the Japanese were incapable of posing a real threat. When Pearl Harbor occurred, Americans realized that they had completely misunderstood not just the particular danger of Japan but the danger of the world in general. As the American fleet sank at Pearl Harbor, the Japanese occupied the Philippines and swept through the western Pacific while the United States was helpless. The United States realized that by being overconfident, it had badly miscalculated. The shock of Pearl Harbor moved the United States from confidence in its power, and the belief in the protection of distance, into a nation on constant alert, searching for the next enemy, and committed to not repeating the mistake of Pearl Harbor.

That made the Soviet Union more than an adversary. It was a persistent existential threat. This might not have been an incorrect view, but the view did not arise from a dispassionate analysis of the reality. The United States now had a compulsion to assume the worst, to believe that the enemy was brilliant and dangerous and could only be defeated by the full force of the nation. The United States was right in treating the Stalinist Soviet Union this way, but it was the way it would treat any adversary after Pearl Harbor.

Pearl Harbor created a sense of dread of the danger that can crop up anywhere. It legitimized and demanded all U.S. efforts to constantly be prepared for the worst. World War II did not create the foreign entanglements in which America has found itself. What it created was a dread of not being constantly entangled so that dangers could be identified and crushed early. It also generated in some Americans a fear of the government itself, of conspiracies and groups that were rumored to control the government. Out of Pearl Harbor was generated the conspiracy theory that Roosevelt not only knew of the Japanese attack but made certain that no one stopped it so that he could justify entering World War II. The sense of dread and the fear of conspiracies were part of the same shift.

After World War II, the president was constantly followed by an officer carrying the nuclear codes, which the president, at his discretion, could employ as he wished. This symbolized the change. According to the Constitution, Congress had to authorize wars by a declaration or by explicit resolutions. But given the nature of nuclear war, such authorization was impractical. Therefore, just as war was becoming more apocalyptic, Congress was marginalized. The president assumed a role much greater than one branch of government among three.

This change extended to the creation of a permanent intelligence establishment after World War II. It was more than an intelligence service, collecting intelligence and analyzing it. It was also engaged in covert operations, under the control of the president. The president had assumed an extraordinarily powerful role. During the Cold War, the United States developed a massive military until about 1970, using conscription. This had never been the case in American history. The industrial side of the military-industrial complex that Eisenhower had warned against also became mammoth and in all practical terms under the control of the federal government. During the Korean War, Harry Truman went to war without any authorization of Congress. The Cuban missile crisis was a purely presidential decision, as was the 1998 intervention in Kosovo. The congressional role in authorizing war was at least diminished and sometimes omitted.

From December 7, 1941, to December 31, 1991, almost fifty years to the day, the United States was in a state of permanent war and near war. Of the fifty years, about fourteen were spent in actual warfare (World War II, Korea, and Vietnam). The other thirty-six years were spent on hair-trigger alert for possible nuclear war with the Soviets. When a human being is constantly in conflict or on alert, the adrenaline alters him. In the case of the United States, in addition to a perpetual anxiety, there was a hunger for secrecy, the creation of massive institutions to manage the vast military and defense industrial apparatus, and the institution of military service as a commonplace event in everyday life. But adrenaline does not only pump you up; it also exhausts you.

During this period, the United States developed a massive intelligence and security service, an enormous standing military, and a large industrial system supporting both. On top was a president with greater powers than ever envisioned by the founders, and a federal presence in American society that was less than during World War II but greater than before the war. This is not an argument that it was bad or unfortunate. Given the nature of World War II, this evolution was inevitable. Given the nature of the Cold War, some version of the World War II model would have to be maintained. The United States had to shift to a wartime preparedness, which gave the president extraordinary power in two ways. First, he had, in practice, authority he didn't have before. Second, he had assets at his disposal he didn't have previously.

Inevitably, the United States affected vast areas of the world and, in so doing, generated both hostility and a desire to align with the United States. But there was no empire of intent, no plan to dominate the world. On the contrary, the overriding impulse was to avoid extensive involvement or, when involved, to focus on spreading American values, rather than establish a system of exploitation.

The United States has little reason to build an empire for economic and trade purposes. It exports only 13 percent of its GDP to the world, compared with Germany, which exports almost 50 percent, or China's exports in excess of 20 percent of GDP. At the same time, the United States is the largest importer in the world, although its imports are only 15 percent of its GDP. The point here is that foreign trade is useful to the United States, but not so useful as to need to impose an empire to assure it. It does not have to require massive imports, nor is it vulnerable to fluctuations in its exports. Indeed, rather than seeking to lock in trade agreements, the United States tends to want to leave, or renegotiate, those agreements, as we have seen during NAFTA and the China trade negotiations.

The economic motive for empire isn't there. Nevertheless, without intention, the American economy is so large and so dynamic that it is constantly affecting the rest of the world. A technical evolution in an American consumer product causes producers around the world to retool their factories. A shift in the American diet can have immense and far-reaching consequences. It can cause massive displacement of sugar or corn growers; it can encourage the planting of quinoa.

In this sense, the United States constantly affects and irritates the world. Even more, the United States affects and irritates the world with its culture. American culture is both disruptive and irreverent. It does not respect precedent or tradition. Yet it is also profoundly attractive to others. Traditionalists around the world—including those in the United States—therefore resent it. The tradition of much of the world revolves around religion and family, and the culture of the United States disrupts both. In the Islamic world, but also in many other places, the presence of American culture is perceived as intending to undermine traditions, the family, and thereby the society as a whole.

The United States sees this happening and in some ways applauds it. It sees young people around the world living under tyranny and listening to American rap music on an iPhone, and the United States assumes that what will happen is the substitution of liberal democracy for tyranny. The spread of technology and music subverts culture, and it is assumed that it will bring other American values along with it. This rarely happens, but it does reveal the persistence in the belief that the transformation and the adoption of American values are desirable. It is no surprise the United States is resented. It is also no surprise that in poll after poll, when citizens of foreign countries are asked what country they would rather live in if they left their own, the United States is always the overwhelming choice.

Empires are resented and hated. They are also admired and envied. They define the culture of the world. By this definition, the United States is an empire. English has become the global language of business and government, and it has become an expectation that professionals around the world will speak English. I have been at meetings where the United States was vehemently condemned by foreign experts and politicians speaking English. The British opened the door to the use of English, but the Americans have taken it much further. The fact that American power exists without any formal structure indicates that the United States is more powerful than most empires have been, historically. Its empire is not only global but casual. It has and uses power casually, controlling the world without a clear plan or even a systematic intent.

The United States has entered a paradoxical period. The basic institutions that had been created during World War II and the Cold War remain in place, if somewhat diminished. The military continues to maintain a large standing army, the intelligence community continues to function, the National Security Council remains operational, and the president's shadow, carrying the nuclear codes, continues to follow him around. In Cheyenne Mountain, in Colorado Springs, the 24-7 watch of the skies continues, looking for something, but not at all clear what it is looking for. The United States could have shut down Cheyenne Mountain. It did not. Endless watching for attack has become institutionalized.

The core problem was inevitable. The United States did not expect the end of the Cold War and had not planned for it. It was left in an enormously powerful position and was uncertain of what to do about it. In the 1980s, it had been one thing. In 1992, it was a very different thing. It was easier to imagine that life would go on as it had been, institutions unchanged, and fantasize that the world would welcome the United States, its economic model, its military power, its technology, and its culture with open arms.

There was an indication that it might be so. As the Soviet Union was collapsing, Saddam Hussein invaded Kuwait and was in a position to threaten the Saudi oil fields. The Americans inserted troops to protect Saudi Arabia and then did something extraordinary. The United States rallied a coalition of thirty-nine countries, with twenty-eight of them sending military forces, to push Iraq out of Kuwait. It was a moment redolent of the United Nations or the League of Nations. The United States willed the coalition into existence almost overnight. It behaved as the leader of the world and it was the leader.

On September 11, 2001, the fantasy blew up. The attack actually started, invisible to the United States, in the American defense of Saudi Arabia during the war with Iraq. Islamic fundamentalists regarded the American presence in the country where Mecca and Medina were located as a sacrilege. Desert Storm was one of the forces generating jihadist anger at the United States. Instead of expecting an age of world peace, it was thrust back into war.

Psychologically, September 11 was on the order of Pearl Harbor. It came out of nowhere, organized by a force that most Americans hadn't heard of before, resurrecting the fears we saw in *High Noon*. The American response was to send a multidivisional force into Afghanistan, where the attack against the United States had been organized. This was followed by a multidivisional invasion of Iraq and smaller attacks in other countries. In others words, the United States, in spite of the lesson in Vietnam, deployed a conventional force to fight a guerrilla war.

Managing an empire means using minimum force, because a global empire is likely to be constantly at war if its first response is to use its own military. The primary strategy for empires is to use diplomacy or the military of others, rather their own. Arming those forces, and giving them political or economic inducements to fight, at least contains the problem without involving imperial forces. The British controlled India with relatively few British troops, using this technique. Over the course of a century, the British used large-scale military force rarely. When they used it against America, they failed. When they later used it in the Boer War, they struggled to succeed. The British reserved their forces as the last resort, which rarely occurred. They managed the empire with local forces willing to fight for British interests for their own reasons.

The United States must expect hostile attacks. Its power will generate hatred, and it should expect neither sympathy nor gratitude. Great, global powers don't get either. The expectation that the United States will be loved as it was after World War I is the expectation of an immature power. Those who want admiration from the world fail to understand what the United States has become and can't back out of.

The American inclination to use its own military force to deal with an entity like al-Qaeda is irrational. That isn't because it is unjust to go to war with al-Qaeda but because the United States cannot fight a war for eighteen years, focusing on one area of the world and neglecting other areas just as important—or more so—to the United States.

The great danger to an empire is permanent war. Given global interests, something is always on fire. If the primary response is war, the empire will always be at war. And if it is always at war somewhere, it will always be vulnerable to someone taking advantage of the empire's preoccupation. Even more important, if the empire doesn't benefit its citizens, but instead exhausts them and disrupts their lives by war, the political support for the empire will quickly evaporate. Both Rome and Britain survived by using minimal direct force, in favor of other means of managing their empires.

The problem is that the United States is emotionally and institutionally designed, since Pearl Harbor, to respond to attack with massive force (even if inappropriate or insufficient to the mission). More than that, it is organized to focus on a response to that particular threat, rather than dissipate its attention. In World War II, it was Germany and Japan. In the Cold War, it was the Soviet Union and China. In both cases, it viewed the rest of the world through the prism of a primary threat. So, if there was a problem in Africa and the Soviets were not involved, the United States didn't respond. If the Soviets were there, the United States became obsessed. This was usually the point where it violated its moral principles unnecessarily, allying with regimes that were distasteful to the United States and of only marginal importance. With a total focus on a single enemy, all other considerations, strategic or moral, became secondary at best.

The Islamic war is the first war the United States has fought as an empire, but it has fought it as if it were simply a great power. It has fought it with an obsessed focus, with primarily its own troops, neglecting its other global interests, and with the lack of subtlety in finding alternatives to take their place. The United States had not yet made the transition from the country that dealt with World War II or with the Cold War to a self-aware empire. It had not made the transition from a great power with important but limited interests to the largest empire that ever existed.

Institutionally, the United States doesn't know how to decline combat. Military force is too frequently used to solve problems that are beyond the ability of the military to solve. The decision-making structure in Washington is complex, diffuse, and at odds with itself. It has streamlined itself not for routine decisions but primarily for crises. Thus, anything that must be dealt with must be elevated to crisis level or the system freezes. Efficient decision making beneath the crisis level is rare. And for an empire, every challenge cannot mean war, and every sub-crisis issue cannot make efficient decision making impossible.

The pressure this brings on the federal government is enormous, and this pressure will play a role in the problems that are arising now, and will intensify in the 2020s. The entire shape of the budget and staff is shifting toward the management of an empire the United States doesn't want to have. Pressure makes the government less efficient and impacts the social and economic dynamic. It's not surprising that nearly two decades of war, and the outmoded shape of a federal government that has had to cope with it, have inevitably contributed to the cyclical crises we will be facing in the 2020s–2030s.

6

The Institutional
Cycles and War

The United States was born in battle. Its institutions were forged in war. Every eighty years or so, the United States shifts the way its political institutions work. The broad framework of the Constitution stays in place, but the federal and state institutions change their relationship to each other and change the way in which they work. So far there have been three such shifts. Each was made necessary because the existing arrangements no longer worked. Triggered by the extreme conditions of war, the institutional structure revealed its weakness and required a new institutional system to replace the old one. And as I will show, we are close to a new institutional shift, forced by the inability of the system to deal with new realities and forged in the conflicts and uncertainty created by the emergence of the United States as the sole global power.

The three previous cycles have been distinct. The first started with the drafting of the Constitution in 1787 and emerged from the Revolutionary War and its consequences. This first institutional cycle lasted seventy-eight years until the end of the Civil War and the amendments to the Constitution in 1865, establishing the federal government but leaving its relation to the states unclear. The second institutional cycle emerged in 1865 from the Civil War and established the authority of the federal government over the states, lasting until the end of World War II. The third institutional cycle began in 1945, emerging from World War II, and dramatically expanded the authority of the federal government not only over states but over the economy and society as a whole.

If this pattern continues as it has, the next institutional cycle will begin around 2025. The coming fourth cycle will redefine the relationship of the federal government to itself. So that we can understand what this next cycle will look like, both as it is taking place and as it defines the next eighty years, we need to understand the previous cycles and the manner in which American invention and reinvention work in this framework.

Eighty years is actually a very short period of time in a nation's history. Other countries have changed in a slower and much less orderly and predictable way. As we have seen, the United States is different, and the core of that difference is that it is an artifact, an invented country. Invention is embedded in all parts of American culture, from technology to society. Other countries, like Russia and Vietnam, are not invented, or if they were invented, it was so long ago that they have developed a different core. When these countries reach a point where the way they operate no longer works, they might flounder, be paralyzed, or fall into chaos. Their core becomes inflexible. The United States metabolizes change differently. In American cities, giant buildings are constructed and torn down within decades. Invention, not tradition, is cherished. The roughly eighty-year periods between the American Revolution and the Civil War, and between the Civil War and World War II, are perhaps accidental. Still, that number is real and I think too odd to be a coincidence. Part of the reason was the speed at which American society was designed to evolve, and part of it was that the federal government was intimately related to war.

Constitutionally, the primary function of the federal government is to assure national security. The president is also the commander in chief of the armed forces. From the beginning many powers remained with the states. One that was reserved for the federal government was waging foreign wars. Inevitably, as the political forces that led to war and the manner in which wars were waged shifted, the institutions of the federal government had to shift as well. Many other things drove and influenced how the nation's institutions evolved, but the central driver remained war.

Let's compare the amount of time the United States spent at war in the last few centuries. In the twentieth century, it was involved in major wars such as World War I and World War II and Vietnam for 17 percent of the time. In the nineteenth century, the percentage was higher. Conventional wars took up about 21 percent of the century, including the War of 1812, the Mexican War, the Civil War, and the Spanish-American War. However, when we include the war against Indian nations, it comes close to 100 percent of the time. And to this point the United States has been at war for almost 100 percent of the twenty-first century. All wars aren't equal. The Civil War and World War II placed unique stress on the nation, as has the long war in the Middle East coupled with terrorism and America's new role in the world.

All wars place stress on a nation's institutions, but some break them. They break them because, as with the Civil War, the war itself is about the relationship between the institutions, or they break them because the war cannot be fought without transforming the nation's institutions. That was the case with World War II. It is not surprising that the United States has frequently been in conflict. Its very creation challenged the British Empire and the European system in general. It also challenged the North American nations, Indian and European. Not all wars transformed institutions, but when social and economic stresses collided with the stress of war, the result was institutional failure—and ultimately a reinvention of the way the country worked.

—

But another, even more significant international event has also taken place. It was not a war but a redefinition of what it meant to be an American and the institutionalization of a constant global presence. American power means constant entanglement in affairs around the world, any one of which might become a war. The only global power must be present throughout the world, not because it wishes, but because the mere size of its economy and military makes this the reality. This creates constant interaction with most of the countries in the world, and conflict with some. During the Cold War, the United States knew the Soviet Union was a potential enemy. Today, potential enemies proliferate not because of anything the United States does but because of who the United States is.

This changes not only U.S. foreign policy but the institutional structure of the United States. The entire world is a potential antagonist and requires constant management. U.S. institutions and the public perception of what it means to be an American must adjust, which is both a difficult and an extended process. But as we've seen with all the cycles, war and the constant pressure of war compel institutional change. What must happen now is an emergence of a mature and restrained pattern of behavior in America's relation to the rest of the world.

Because I believe we are approaching the end of the current institutional cycle and the beginning of the fourth, it may help to try to understand in greater detail what led to the end of the second cycle and how the current, third cycle arose.

The Fall of the Second Institutional Cycle

After the Civil War, it was established that the federal government had ultimate authority over the states. It was a limited authority, but strong enough to establish an indivisible republic. But it was a republic of great distances and diversity. New Mexico was

THE STORM BEFORE THE CALM

very different from Maine, and the practical ability of the federal government, with limited resources to directly govern both, was impossible. The federal government's power rested in its capability to enforce the Constitution and to limit the sovereignty of the states to self-government within that framework. Given what the Articles of Confederation had said, and what the Constitution left uncertain, this created a new institutional period in which there was one country, indivisible. But the federal government did not involve itself with the private lives of individuals or, for the most part, with the functioning of private property, particularly business. As the second cycle proceeded, the wall began to break down, but the institutions collapsed because of two things.

First in 1929, the Great Depression began the process of challenging the institutional framework of the second cycle. The Depression posed a profound problem. Unless it was managed, it would certainly lead to social unrest or even an uprising. Many were desperate, and desperation can threaten institutions. The only way the federal government could manage this problem was to break out of the existing institutional framework and intervene in the economy.

When Franklin Roosevelt was elected president, he was committed to solving the problem but gave no hint of how he would do it. He seemed to have no clear idea or plan. Trapped by circumstances, he started to shift the relationship of government and society. The Depression created an economic failure that turned into a social and political crisis. Factories that were able to manufacture products faced consumers who could not buy them, because they were unemployed. That led to closing more factories, in a downward spiral. During past depressions, of which there were several, the federal government kept its distance. But there were two things that made this crisis different.

First was its intensity and longevity. When President Roosevelt took office in 1933, the Depression had been raging for more than three years, with no sign of letup. The second problem was that society had become much more complex. An agrarian society of small farm holders is relatively simple. Economic downturns disrupt society, but farms produce food, and that food is enough to get by on. The industrial society of the 1930s depended on cities, where vast numbers of workers lived, and where factories were clustered, to form a supply chain. In cities, depressions strike with a vengeance. Hunger wasn't far off. Getting people back to work, or at least getting them relief, was a political imperative.

The federal government faced a problem. The adherents of the second institutional cycle argued that the government reducing taxes and avoiding involvement in the economy and society could solve the Depression. This was the foundation of the second cycle. But that situation, if it worked in the long run, would increase pressure on the economy, and even if the discipline worked, its timing and that of the political clock were out of sync. Given the pressures both on the working class and on the industrial plant, simply allowing nature to take its course was not viable. Radical political movements like Huey Long's Share Our Wealth or the Communists were not really powerful, but given time and enough pain, they would become so.

Economic and political considerations required a solution, and the only conceivable way to solve the problem was intervening in society and the economy. Hunting for ways to pay at least some of the unemployed, Roosevelt introduced legislation raising the maximum tax rate to 75 percent. In theory, this should have worked. The problem was the United States had an industrial plant that outstripped the demand for its goods. Increasing the tax rate cut back on investable income and meant that plants would not increase their capacity and that cash would be diverted to consumption. But no one was investing in industrial plants, and little of the money taken in taxes went into the hands of the unemployed. The New Deal didn't end the Depression, but it established the principle that the federal government was in some way responsible for the economy and could legitimately intervene in the economy and society.

What did solve the problem, ended the Depression, and finally broke the institutions of the second cycle was war. The essence of American strategy in World War II was industrial production. Building 300,000 aircraft, 6,000 ships, and almost 200,000 tanks would win the war. The United States mobilized twelve million men and women for military service who had to be fed, clothed, and housed. Munitions had to be produced, items like barbed wire had to be manufactured, and medical equipment of all types had to be produced. To generate all this, a vast swath of the economy was contracted to the war effort. And in the process of contracting, raw materials like oil, steel, and copper had to be rationed, not only to the civilian population, but to the various factories. The federal government had to set the priorities and apportion raw materials based on those priorities.

Industrial production in such massive quantity and at such a fast pace solved the problem of unemployment. The war also broke down many barriers between public and private life and changed private life as well, with women and African Americans being permitted into roles that had previously been barred to them. The greatest barrier that was broken was the barrier between the federal government and business. Business thrived on federal contracts, but in turn was managed to an extraordinary extent by the federal government.

The complexity of fighting the war and aligning the economy with the needs of the military required a management system large enough to administer the breadth and complexity of the economy and the government that oversaw them. Many of these managers were in the military, and many officers were recruited from business to oversee various aspects of the process. But the federal government grew as well. Driven by the necessities of war, the integration of the federal government with the economy and society surged. And looking back on it, the period was relatively well managed because the managers were inventing solutions and did not see themselves as in more than temporary jobs.

After World War II, the federal government retreated. Things like rationing were eliminated; the size of the military shrank. And government contracts did not dominate the economy. But the government engagement with private life did not go away, with the military driving much of that engagement at first. An example of how the wartime system turned into a peacetime reality is the manner in which military requirements shaped technology, drawing in scientists and corporations both in producing the technologies and then in turning them into consumer products as well as military ones.

The Great Depression rendered the second institutional cycle obsolete. The institutional rules that were in place did not solve the problem, and the problem had to be solved. World War II took the New Deal to its most extreme conclusion, by intertwining the federal government in both the economy and the society. With both having essentially been nationalized during World War II, the older model was abandoned, and the foundation of a new institutional cycle was established and would remain in place for the next eighty years.

To get a sense of the depths of the federal government's power, let's consider what happened during World War II with the government's relationship to the sciences. The single most dramatic example of this alliance was the Manhattan Project. Scientists discovered the basic principles of nuclear fission in universities. With the outbreak of the war, they presented the military with the possibility of building an atomic bomb. The military organized the scientists and tied them to business, whose industrial capacity and other expertise would be needed to produce the bomb. The Manhattan Project succeeded, and the standing of scientists was elevated in the minds of citizens, the military, and the federal government. They were the foundation of America's victory.

The Manhattan Project was one of many such projects that succeeded in World War II. But the success of the Manhattan Project riveted the nation. It was a project so startling and defining that it became a model for the next cycle. The Manhattan Project could only have existed with federal money, organization, and compulsion. It had to be an absolute secret, and the federal government controlled the lives of the workers and hid the project from its citizens. All this was necessary, yet all this changed how America worked. The federal government could shape industry without being answerable to society, yet the technology developed would change the everyday lives of people.

In this way, the military gained the technology it needed to fight the Cold War. Scientists and other scholars had the opportunity to pursue research they otherwise could not have done. Corporations received government contracts and the opportunity to repurpose technology for the public. Yet it was the government that shaped the evolution of science and technology.

In the prior institutional cycle, the practice had been that science and technology were the purviews of universities and corporations. Thomas Edison was the embodiment of the corporate exploitation of science, and as we have seen, he was dramatically successful. He was also a committed pacifist who opposed the use of his work by the military. This practice didn't work in World War II, because it was too diffuse and unpredictable. In a war, focus and predictability were essential. Therefore, federal departments organized universities and their scientists and corporations and their engineers into a single, federally funded enterprise, and they were not pacifists.

In one sense, the founders did envision federal involvement in science. The Northwest Ordinance, which defined how American territories might become states and was drafted by Thomas Jefferson, mandated that every new state set aside land for the creation of a university. The principle was there from the beginning, but it evolved in ways that were unanticipated. Universities, the federal government, and private industry combined during this period to transform private life.

This model is still very much in place. Look at the smartphone. The cell phone was first deployed for the U.S. Army in 1985. The National Reconnaissance Office first designed the camera in the smartphone for use in spy satellites. The GPS function on a cell phone was first devised and implemented by the U.S. Air Force, lithium-ion batteries were developed by the Department of Energy, and the Internet was pioneered by the Defense Advanced Research Projects Agency. So what you have in the smartphone is a compendium of military hardware, much of it researched in universities and turned into weapons and products by corporations. Because federal inventions can't be patented, companies like Apple took the technology and developed the smartphone. Science, industry, and the federal government, particularly the military, combined to drive the American economy. It was in the relationship between the federal government and a redefinition of institutions that we can see the triumph and failure of the system.

This model won World War II, making the United States one of two global superpowers. The model also ended the Depression and permitted the continued and dramatic growth of the country. The federal government's relation to private life changed in World War II. It was central to winning the war, because World War II was won or lost on the ability to utilize the industrial base. That meant binding together the various elements of industrial society into an integrated and managed whole. In effect, the federal government took control of the economy, allocating raw material and dictating what could and couldn't be produced and how it would be distributed.

America's institutions and society after World War II were very different from what they were at the start of the war. This was the end of the second institutional cycle, and America was reshaping itself once again.

The Third Institutional Cycle

The idea that emerged from both the New Deal and World War II was that a state managed by experts dedicated to solutions without an ideology would do for the country what it did for the war: it would breed success. But of course, this became a principle, the principle became a belief, and the belief became an ideology. The ideology created a class who felt entitled to govern and who were believed to be suitable to govern.

It brought scientists a degree of power, but this class comprised not only government experts. There were corporate experts and academic experts, graduates of journalism schools, business schools, and law schools. It had once been possible to sit on the Supreme Court having never gone to law school. Now Supreme Court justices were legal experts, rather than people chosen for their wisdom. The financial community was controlled by experts. Technocracy is the concept that emerged early in the twentieth century that argues that government should be in the hands of nonideological and apolitical experts whose power derived from their knowledge. Technocracy was not primarily about wealth. It was about merit regardless of the rewards. Thus, tech billionaires and assistant professors held the same core belief in expertise and merit and above all the credentials that certified these things—degrees from the right schools. As we will see, technocracy plays a vital role in our current and in future cycles.

The focus of the technocracy was social engineering, restructuring the way in which economic and social institutions worked in order to improve the lives of citizens. This was not unprecedented. The system of distribution of land in the western territories during the first institutional cycle certainly reengineered society. What made this different was the construction of deeply organized systems that interacted with the economy and society as a whole. There is a vast difference between granting land to settlers and creating a financial system for home ownership, which in turn changed the landscape of America.

Veterans returned from World War II as a favored class. Many married and wanted to have their own homes, but they lacked the money for a down payment. The federal government stepped in and guaranteed the loans, and they were made with no money down and at low interest rates. It gave the veterans a just reward and stimulated the economy. It was a conceptually simple program, unprecedented in its intrusion into what had previously been something managed in the private sphere, between lender and borrower. But the program followed the principles of the new cycle and had far-reaching effects in helping to create the postwar middle class. In tracing its course, we can also see how it led to the crisis of 2008.

The veterans' mortgages would mean building houses, and the houses required land. They couldn't be built in already crowded cities that had no available land. Nor could they build them far away from the cities because the workers had to commute daily to jobs in the city. The result was the creation of suburbs encircling cities, and the suburbs of course needed roads connecting them to the city and to each other. And the suburbs needed stores to sell things required by the people living there, and parking lots in which to park. New school systems had to be built, as well as houses of worship and hospitals and other services.

The federal government, in wanting to provide homes to returning veterans, changed American society to the core. We can debate whether this was an improvement, but what cannot be denied was that it happened. And while the technocrats had planned meticulously and successfully for providing veterans with homes, it was the unintended consequences that towered over their efforts. This was a dimension of social engineering and the expertise of technocrats. When the projects failed, resources were wasted. When they succeeded, it resembled Mickey Mouse as the Sorcerer's Apprentice—unintentionally unleashing all sorts of forces. The ideology of expertise failed to take into account that the expert's narrow focus prevented him—and other people—from anticipating what they had opened the door to.

In this case, the growth of the suburbs intensified with similar programs that intertwined with other American realities. The VA loan concept was extended to lower-income home buyers who had not been veterans. It was managed by the Federal Housing Administration and allowed the lower-middle class to buy homes. The program was a great success, and it was decided that the banks holding them could sell these guaranteed mortgages to investors, increasing money available for lending. This increase of available money delighted the construction industry, home buyers, and banks.

The instrument used was the Federal National Mortgage Association, Fannie Mae, a government-created entity that handled failed mortgages in the Depression in order to stabilize banks. Fannie Mae (and a later cousin, Freddie Mac) bought mortgages from banks in order to maintain the availability of mortgage money. Banks basically made their money off processing mortgages. The mortgages were sold and the risk transferred to these entangled, half-government and half-private entities, Fannie Mae and Freddie Mac. Because Fannie Mae's original job was handling troubled loans, and the FHA was guaranteeing loans made to buyers who wouldn't ordinarily qualify for mortgages, and because the mortgages were sold to Fannie Mae, everyone was comfortable—realtors, developers, home buyers, banks.

As we move from the 1950s to the 1970s and then to 2008, we notice a problem. A perfectly good idea morphed into another good idea, spread beyond housing, and then culminated in uncontrolled insanity. By 2008, no one, including the management of Fannie

Mae and Freddie Mac or the Department of Housing and Urban Development, had any idea of the fragility of their own institutions. The knowledge could have been obtained, but it would have been enormously complicated to do so. Government insurance gave the illusion of invulnerability, and a capable system of management was never built. The federal government created these entities, and no elected official had the capacity to monitor them. By this time, the matter had become far more complicated, with private institutions buying mortgages as well and selling derivatives on the mortgages, with no one being able to tell whether the people who borrowed the money could pay it back.

The purpose here is not to track the details of the subprime crisis. It is to make the point that this started as a very reasonable program to help veterans. It turned into a program to help the lower-middle class while also aiding business. What followed was giving banks the ability to sell mortgages, which over the decades both introduced private buyers of mortgages and made lenders pretty much indifferent to the creditworthiness of borrowers. In due course, it ended in disaster. As we can now see, these disasters took decades to work themselves through.

The institutional problem was not that the government had grown too large. In fact, relative to population, it has not kept up. The number of government employees has doubled since 1940, but the population has more than doubled, from 139 million to 320 million. The government with the greatest increases in staffing is not the federal government but local and state governments. During this same period, government employment outside the military has stayed steady. Some facts are worth noting. The federal government's last growth spurt was during the Reagan administration.

There is also a strong concern that the size of the federal debt (and consumer debt as well) will have calamitous effects on the economy. The idea, not unreasonable, is that debt eventually reaches

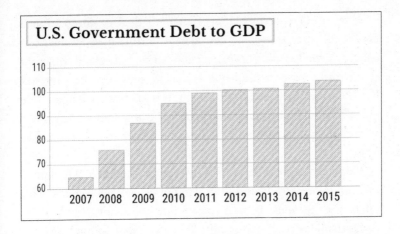

U.S. Government Debt to GDP

a point where it can't be repaid. This fear has been current since the Great Depression, when the public learned to fear the irresponsibility of all institutions. But the fact is that as the debt has risen since World War II, during the 1980s and beyond, the fears of collapse, hyperinflation, and the rest have not been realized. The common answer is, no matter, it will happen. That might be true, but a more likely explanation for the lack of disaster can be glimpsed in the next chart.

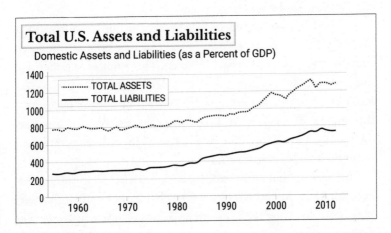

Total U.S. Assets and Liabilities

Domestic Assets and Liabilities (as a Percent of GDP)

When the creditworthiness of an individual or corporation is examined, three things are considered: indebtedness, annual revenue, and total assets. For reasons difficult to understand, when the creditworthiness of a country is evaluated, only one year's revenue (GDP) is measured against total debt. It is as if the total of an individual's debt, from home mortgage, car loans, and student debt, were measured against one year's income. Obviously, that would be irrational.

Think about the situation of a billionaire who has $50 million of income one year and has $100 million of debt. If you ignore he is a billionaire, he would be in desperate financial shape. If you add in his assets, he is very comfortable. When you look at the chart, you can see that American assets, very conservatively measured, vastly outstrip debt. The United States is like the billionaire with debt larger than this year's income but well within his means to handle. Obviously, the same ratio of GDP to debt for different countries will have very different outcomes. Some countries collapse under this level of debt because of limited assets. As an example, think of Iceland in 2008, when its three major banks—Glitnir, Landsbanki, and Kaupthing—had a systemic collapse, causing a severe depression in the country for several years.

The problem of the federal government is not its indebtedness or its size. That can be shown by the fact that none of the long-standing prophecies have been fulfilled. The problem is rather that the dramatically increasing level of federal involvement in society has outstripped its institutional capabilities. This is the reason that the national debt has not had the consequence that many were predicting since the 1980s. The problem with the federal government is not financial. It is institutional.

The institutional crisis is rooted in two things. First, the governing class, and the technocrats, accumulate power and wealth, and they begin to shape the institutions to protect their interests. The second problem is that the expertise that won World War II and built the postwar world is now encountering its own problem of inefficiency—diffusion.

Diffusion is the distribution of authority among several departments or agencies. At a lower level, it is the diffusion and fragmentation of knowledge among individual experts. Knowledge of what is happening is diffused rather than integrated. Diffusion ties in with the problem of expertise. Expertise is needed. But experts are experts in different things, and when entities are constructed with specific expertise, barriers are built between entities that are sometimes dealing with the same issue. Instead of creating a single perspective on a problem, experts have perspectives on different parts of a problem, and the entity they represent has parallel responsibilities for fragments of an issue. This creates diffusion with the federal government and frequently contradictory directions for entities. What had begun in World War II as an effort that was highly focused on war and tightly controlled turned into a highly diffused undertaking frequently lacking a center from which it can be understood. This is not unique to the federal government. It happens in all, particularly large, organizations. Expertise has this inherent defect. But in the federal government, the problem is the size of the defect.

The other problem is entanglement, multiple federal agencies engaged in managing parts of the same problem. One form of entanglement is that of the various agencies, which battle each other for funding and turf. The Administrative Conference of the United States lists 115 agencies of the federal government but notes,

There is no authoritative list of government agencies. . . . For example, FOIA.gov [maintained by the Department of Justice] lists 78 independent executive agencies and 174 components of the executive departments as units that comply with the Freedom of Information Act requirements imposed on every federal agency. This appears to be on the conservative end of the range of possible agency definitions. The *United States*

Government Manual lists 96 independent executive units and 220 components of the executive departments. An even more inclusive listing comes from USA.gov, which lists 137 independent executive agencies and 268 units in the Cabinet.

There are so many entities within entities that it is impossible to count them all.

The entanglement of various agencies with each other is compounded by a massive entanglement with society. The barrier having been broken, there are few areas of private life in which the federal government is not in some way involved. Health care, education at all levels, agriculture, transportation, managing international trade, virtually any significant area of private life is somehow bound up with the federal government, either as regulator or as major consumer. And there is hardly any area where only a single agency is involved. The entanglement between agencies becomes the defining characteristic of the federal system.

As society became more complex in its own right, and the federal imperative to try to manage this growing complexity tries to keep pace, management becomes more complex, regulations are created that are less comprehensible, and authority is less clearly defined.

The institutional crisis has been building since the maturation of the third cycle. As with the first two cycles, what started as splendid ideas eventually wore out as the society changed. What is going on, at root, is a basic asymmetry between the federal government as it was conceived of in 1945 and the economy and society today. Huge corporations and an industrial workforce filled the landscape then, and the social problem was exploiting the surplus wealth that was created in World War II. We now face a very different social and economic crisis, as we will discuss in the next chapter.

Another important aspect of the third institutional cycle is that the balance of the three federal powers has changed. Probably the most obvious is that the power of the president has increased dramatically. His formal powers have not increased, but his weight in the overall system has. Partly it was to do with domestic affairs, a result of his ability to interpret the meaning of laws in the course of writing regulations and administering the law. The second and the real impetus to the rest was the shift in his powers in foreign policy.

Nuclear weapons and the Cold War introduced a technical problem. Nuclear war operates with a speed that prevents the president from consulting with Congress. In the event of nuclear war, the president had to have the power to immediately don the mantle of commander in chief without a declaration of war or a resolution from Congress as required by the Constitution. He had an implicit resolution to wage war as he chose. Indeed, he was not only free to respond to a Soviet attack but free to initiate war.

This was then extended to conventional war. No war since World War II was waged with a declaration of war, and many began without even a congressional resolution. The Korean War had no congressional involvement because President Truman claimed that since the UN Security Council had declared a police action, and the United States was part of the UN, waging war in Korea required no congressional approval. It was the first war of any size without congressional approval. The same was true in Vietnam, where President Lyndon Johnson claimed that the Gulf of Tonkin Resolution, which did not address the question of whether a multiyear, multidivisional war might be waged, was authorization for the war in which fifty thousand Americans died. During the Cuban missile crisis, the question of what ought to be done was decided by the president and his advisers, without formal or even informal congressional approval.

The increase in presidential power has been seen during the current jihadist wars of the last eighteen years in a more extreme way. The president claimed the authority to conduct surveillance on American citizens' telephone activities and other collective communications. Many of the aspects of the program were secret and not known to Congress at all. The president claimed in his role of commander in chief the right to commence warfare and monitor Americans at his will without congressional approval. The balance of powers has become unhinged.

It was not simply the imperial presidency, a notion that went back to the 1960s. It was the reality of contemporary war. There were minutes to decide on how to deal with a nuclear attack. Korea was attacked on a weekend, and the decision to go to war had to be made then and there. Jihadist operatives were in the United States planning attacks, and surveillance on individuals was one way, if inefficient, of stopping them. The Cuban missile crisis and many before and after could not withstand a congressional debate. Action potentially had to be secret to be effective.

And this further shifted the balance of power. Staffers to the president and experts scattered through the intelligence, defense, and foreign policy communities could affect the decisions being made far more than could Congress. The head of the National Security Council, or the deputy director of the CIA for operations, had more control over U.S. actions and strategy than the Speaker of the House, who was sometimes informed of what would happen but rarely consulted. Secrecy came first, and the apparatus controlled by the president had both the expertise and the discipline to maintain secrecy. Congress did not. Thus in foreign and security policy, the president continually accumulated more and more power in the third cycle. This did not, however, often lead to success.

The crisis is this: institutions built on expertise are no longer working. The federal government is increasingly diffuse and entangled and cannot operate in a timely or efficient manner. Universities are increasingly inefficient, with tuition and student loans at staggering levels, making the cost of acquiring credentials increasingly out of the reach of much of the population. The Internet is increasingly incoherent, and newspapers can no longer maintain needed staff. As for the technocrats of Google and Goldman Sachs, the vast accumulation of money that increasingly could not be efficiently reinvested, but still created a vast gap in wealth that had been alleviated to some extent after World War II, has become a defining characteristic of society.

The accumulation of wealth by experts, combined with the decreasing efficiency of technocracy, is creating this third institutional crisis. But because it's early in the crisis, those who in some way recognize it are still impotent to change it. President Trump came into office promising to "drain the swamp," a metaphor for attacking technocracy, but he had neither the clarity as to how to proceed nor the political base from which to do it. The country was still divided down the middle, with the technocrats successfully defending their institutions.

The third institutional crisis is now in its first stages, driven by the new and uncomfortable position of the United States in the world and the long jihadist wars. The United States is looking for a new framework for dealing with the world, but can't readily do so in the framework of the third institutional cycle. In this cycle, the federal government was constantly engaged in both foreign and domestic matters. That constant entanglement under the guise of management cannot be sustained. We must turn to the second type of cycle, the socioeconomic cycle, which is equally influential on the United States and is concluding at nearly the same time and amplifying the chaos.

7

The Socioeconomic Cycles

American society and the American economy have a rhythm. Every fifty years or so, they go through a painful and wrenching crisis, and in those times it often feels as if the economy were collapsing, and American society with it. Policies that had worked for the previous fifty years stop working, causing significant harm instead. A political and cultural crisis arises, and what had been regarded as common sense is discarded. The political elite insists that there is nothing wrong that couldn't be solved by more of the same. A large segment of the public, in great pain, disagrees. The old political elite, and its outlook on the world, is discarded. New values, new policies, and new leaders emerge. The new political culture is treated with contempt by the old political elite, who expect to return to power shortly, when the public comes to its senses. But only a radically new approach can solve the underlying economic problem. The problem is solved over time, a new common sense is put into place, and America flourishes—until it is time for the next economic and social crisis and the next cycle.

It has been nearly forty years since the last cyclical transition occurred. In 1981, Ronald Reagan replaced Jimmy Carter as president, changing economic policy, political elites, and the common sense that had dominated the United States for the fifty years since

Roosevelt replaced Herbert Hoover. If a pattern that goes back to the founding holds, the United States is due for its next socioeconomic shift in about 2030. But well before that, the underlying exhaustion of the old era will begin to show itself. Political instability will arise a decade or more before the shift, accompanied by growing economic problems and social divisions. When the crisis matures, it concludes with someone who will be regarded as a failed president and with the emergence of a new president who does not create the new cycle but rather permits it to take place. Over the following decade or so, the United States reshapes itself, and the new era emerges.

What has to be remembered is that the political strife and noise are simply the outer wrapping around deep social and economic dislocation. Politics isn't the engine pushing the system. The system is pushing politics. Roosevelt and Reagan didn't found their eras. The era was in crisis, and that crisis could not be solved in conventional ways. A break with the past was essential, and Roosevelt and Reagan presided over what was necessary.

To date there have been five of these socioeconomic cycles. The first began with George Washington and ended with John Quincy Adams. The second began with Andrew Jackson and ended with Ulysses S. Grant. The third began with Rutherford B. Hayes and ended with Herbert Hoover. The fourth began with Franklin Roosevelt and ended with Jimmy Carter. The fifth began with Ronald Reagan and will end with someone whose name we don't know yet, but he or she will likely be elected president in 2028. We have to remember that presidents are simply the street signs. The cycle is working itself out in the murky depths.

The First Socioeconomic Cycle:
The Washington Cycle, 1783–1828

Let's look at the history of socioeconomic cycles. The founding of the United States took place between 1783 with victory in the revolution against England and 1789 with the ratification of the Constitution and the election of George Washington as president. The United States was no longer a group of states without common interests. The revolution transformed the structure of American governance. First the Americans expelled the British, and then they created a framework for that governance. But the revolution was odd in that it was a revolution fomented and controlled by the dominant class, which remained in place and in control after the revolution. Institutionally, the United States was transformed. Socially and economically, it was left intact. Men like Washington, Adams, and Jefferson, the first three presidents, represented the southern aristocracy and the northern business class that dominated the colonies, triggered the revolution, and governed afterward.

After a revolution, stability is essential. The French and Russian Revolutions showed what might happen when a revolution leads to social unrest and economic uncertainty. The first American cycle gave time for the political system to settle into place while maintaining social stability. During the first socioeconomic cycle, the United States was content with its geography, between the Atlantic and the Appalachians, and it was content with its social and ethnic structure. Its domestic economy was mercantile, built around agriculture and the core industries of international trade, shipbuilding, and finance. The system was both revolutionary and stable. It overthrew what went before, yet stability followed rapidly. The juxtaposition of radical change and stable outcome was the mark of this first cycle.

The Industrial Revolution was well under way in England, led by a transformation in the textile industry. England continued to be a threat to the newly formed nation because the United States remained economically locked into trade with England, and England's growing wealth allowed it to build a navy that dominated the Atlantic. British intentions became clear in the War of 1812. A trade war with the British had created a massive depression in America from 1807 to 1809. The United States as a whole could remain in the economic position it was in, but that meant the social structure built on that position could not be sustained. It's interesting that while the cyclical shift was about twenty years away, the problem that would cause the crisis was already becoming visible.

Building dynamism into the American economy in this period had two dimensions. The first was increasing agricultural production. The second was to industrialize the country in order to keep pace economically and militarily with Britain. However, industrialization required a greater capital base and population, and they both had to precede industrialization. The only way to do this was to exploit the land west of the Appalachians. Part of that, the Northwest Territories, was already American. Another part, Louisiana, was purchased in 1803. But neither could be settled without building a network of roads and trails through the Appalachians and finding people who wanted to settle there. This required immigration.

New settlers had increasingly been coming to the United States since the end of the revolution, including Germans, Swedes, and, most important, Scots-Irish. The Scots had been searching for land to farm for centuries. They had settled in Ireland, beginning to arrive in the United States in large numbers in the 1790s and struggling to become independent farmers. They were culturally distinct from and hostile to the English. They were individualists, combative, hard drinking, and hardworking. The English looked down on them and viewed these Presbyterians as a danger to the order the English had created. James Logan, secretary to the Penn family of Pennsylvania, said of the earliest Scots-Irish arrivals that "the settlement of five families of [Scots-Irish] gives me more trouble than fifty of any other people." They were seen as illiterate, violent drunkards, a view that set the pattern for greeting immigrants. Germans soon joined the Scots-Irish. Ben Franklin called the Germans "stupid and swarthy."

But the land had to be settled, and that meant America needed immigrants. Inevitably, new immigrants challenged the stability of society, their arrival changing the economic system to some degree, and the social order substantially. Their poverty and alien culture made them objects of contempt resulting in the creation of deep tensions. While the nation had to have them, the existing social order could not tolerate them.

As the Scots-Irish came to make a home across the Appalachians, they quickly became resentful at the way land in the West was apportioned and sold. They resented the English elite's absentee power just as they resented the English absentee landlords in Scotland. Also, they resented that the political order, which presented itself as a people's government, was actually controlled by a pseudo aristocracy. New immigrants were essential to the development of the United States, attracted to its democratic and even anarchic elements, and viewed those who governed the thirteen original states with the same contempt as the elite regarded them.

The struggle of the settlers to control their land began with a financial crisis. Alexander Hamilton had created the First Bank of the United States. It was privately owned but designed to manage a stable currency. The stresses of the founding, including the war debt from the revolution, caused Congress to allow its charter to lapse. This did not improve the situation, and in 1816 a new charter was created for the Second Bank of the United States. It was also a private bank, owned by wealthy investors. Its task was to manage the money supply of the country by curtailing excessive lending by other banks.

A private bank, operated for profit, being responsible for the prudent management of the money supply, was not a great idea, and, not surprisingly, it didn't work well. While credit was easy to obtain, land prices rose dramatically. The wealth of the earlier settlers surged, while new settlers were forced out of the land market. It also made several investors in the bank quite rich. Speculation in western land became frenzied, and the resulting inflation affected the rest of the country as well.

The settlers felt the bank was being managed to the benefit of the financial community, not in their interests. Then, in Europe in 1819, a financial panic occurred. Banks and businesses had borrowed heavily during the Napoleonic Wars, and a wave of defaults and bankruptcies led to a depression lasting until 1821. The crisis involved the United States because eastern bankers in New York and Boston had invested in European debt, so default heavily damaged the banking sector. The panic drove home the danger of involvement in European finance, and it also illuminated the fragility of the American financial system and therefore the economy. The year 1819 raised reasonable doubts about the prudence of the class that had dominated the nation since the founding. Any argument that the moneyed classes were more prudent didn't mesh with their apparently reckless lending practices. Even more at issue was their heavy investment in Europe rather than in making credit available to new settlers in America. A massive social divide opened up, a political crisis was brewing, and the coming decade would experience turbulence on all levels.

In 1822, the Second Bank of the United States tightened the money supply, which created a double crisis. The value of land in the West plunged. Many of the settler farmers had borrowed against the inflated value of their property and owed more than the land was now worth. New settlers could not get credit from banks to buy land, equipment, or farming supplies. The price of land fell due to lack of credit, yet many settlers were still priced out of the market. This was a threat to the geopolitical strategy of the United States, built on settling the West and attaining strategic depth. On top of this, decreased agricultural production raised food prices in the East. Not surprisingly, the country went into a depression, which, among other things, led to a political debate over the purpose of the Second Bank.

The problem was that the Second Bank had control of the money supply through a complex relationship with other banks. Because the dollars circulated had no backing beyond the word of the Second Bank, and the availability of money had less to do with solving social problems than assuring that the interests of the banking system were protected, the depression that struck the United States lasted several years. It particularly devastated western settlers. The Scots-Irish, who were already seen by the earlier English settlers and bankers as lazy and shiftless, were viewed as being responsible for their condition.

The United States was now reaching the end of its first era. It had to expand westward. It needed food production to surge. Settlers were being crushed by Hamilton's formerly useful and now-harmful idea of how credit ought to be managed. And continuing doing what had worked so well in the first part of the era would intensify the crisis. The core functioning of the financial system had to be changed. But many believed this radical notion needed to be resisted, because the idea that the past is obsolete is always resisted at an era's end. And the next election inevitably produced a presidency that was committed to preserving the past.

The 1824 election came down to a contest between a member of the English elite, John Quincy Adams, and a member of the Scots-Irish lower class, Andrew Jackson. It was the perfect representation of the split in the United States. When cycles enter a transitional phase, political instability and electoral chaos are common. The election of 1824 was perhaps the wildest in American history. Jackson felt that Adams had stolen the election, and he could make a case for that. The Electoral College could not manage to muster a majority, divided as it was over several candidates. It wound up in the House of Representatives, the only election ever to go there, and the deal making was prodigious. Adams won, and the Washington era hung on.

John Quincy Adams's presidency was a disaster. Adams's goal was to preserve the existing financial system. Adams did not understand the new cycle that was beginning. Being the last president of an era means being unable to accommodate the future. The era Adams loved was gone. America had changed since 1776. Part of the change was geopolitical: the land west of the Appalachians had to be settled. Part was ethnic: a new wave of immigrants brought with it a different culture. Part was economic: the approach to the financial policy of the first era could not support new economic realities. The old model was exhausted, and there was no going back. Either a new system would emerge, or the nation would fragment.

The Second Socioeconomic Cycle: The Jackson Cycle, 1828–1876

Andrew Jackson did finally win the election of 1828, the first president from west of the Appalachians. This was the beginning of the process to construct the new cycle. It was the pivot point and not the end of the battle. And the battle was still focused on the banking system.

The Second Bank's charter wasn't due to expire until 1836, and Jackson did not yet have the political power to crush it. If 1828 was the pivot, the transition crisis began around 1819 and lasted until 1836, when the bank was finally dissolved after Jackson's reelection. But until then, there were still economic tremors. Stable money, with stable credit, was needed for the settlement of the West. Jackson supported the call for a dollar backed by both gold and silver. Gold was stable but limited the money supply. Silver was less rare and therefore built expansion into the currency. By linking the dollar to both metals, Jackson hoped to create sufficient liquidity without causing bubbles.

That was in the long run. In the short run, this created the panic of 1837, and the stabilization of the currency resulted in a banking crisis in the United States. This wasn't the only cause of the crisis. The wheat crop in the United States failed in the same year, and there was a massive financial crisis in Britain that affected the United States as well. This does point out two things. First, the actions required to adjust to a new cycle frequently cause economic pain, particularly to those who did not anticipate the changes, believing the old cycle to be eternal. Second, nearly a decade after the presidential shift, the transition was still under way.

Given the importance of the Civil War, it would seem reasonable to assume that it was a turning point in American history. From an institutional point, it certainly was. From the standpoint of economics, there was a great deal of commonality on both sides of the Civil War. Lincoln was a westerner, born in Kentucky and settled in Illinois. He championed the interests of the Union against the South, but he also championed western settlers. He signed the Homestead Act in 1862, which gave 160 acres of federal land in the West to anyone who would farm it for five years. This opened the door to greater settlement of the West and also undermined land speculation by locking in ownership for five years and bringing large amounts of new land to the market.

In this, Lincoln was clearly part of the Jackson cycle. Given his towering importance in American history, it is odd that he would not be a social and economic pivot. However, Lincoln's importance was in the massive institutional shift that took place after the Civil War. From a social and political standpoint, he governed within the framework of Jackson's cycle, settling the land and making it productive. However, he governed toward the end of the cycle in which Grant was the failed president. As I have said before, political instability breaks out a bit more than a decade from the end of a social and economic cycle. Hayes was elected in 1876, and the Civil War broke out fifteen years before that, the mother of all precursors.

However, a new cycle was developing. One of the major issues of the Civil War was the South exporting cotton to Britain, and it could not afford a tariff war. The North was just beginning to industrialize and wanted protection from foreign competition. After the Civil War, the South was broken and industrialization had gotten a powerful boost from the war. But something else happened that had been under way for some time. The agricultural Midwest became the heartland of the country. Its residents now were stable landowners, with small towns having sprung up to service them. Industrialization created radically different cultures in large cities that had previously been financial and commercial centers, not places where massive production took place. Industrialism was changing that.

A financial crisis rooted in the Civil War broke out in 1873, prefacing a change in eras. What led to this crisis? It is logical that financing the Civil War had required massive federal borrowing. When that proved insufficient, the federal government started issuing currency not backed by silver or gold, thus reversing the Jackson model. As a result, the war left the American economy in chaos. Old gold-backed currency was still in circulation, but the government lacked the gold to back it up. Bondholders were being paid in dollars that had little value. Holders of Confederate bonds were wiped out. Gold- and silver-backed dollars were pulled out of the economy as savings. The result was inflation, which people in debt loved but which devastated the creditors. A huge social rift opened, and then the inevitable financial crisis, the one that precedes the end of a cycle, occurred in 1873.

This financial crisis hit shares in railroads, the advanced technology of this era. There had been massive speculation in railroads, and in 1873, as all speculative bubbles do, it burst. The collapse of railroad stocks impacted Europe, which had invested heavily in the

United States. Another major victim was the small-town banker, who had spread all over the West in the communities that had sprouted up to support regional farmers.

Small towns had become the symbol of the virtuous life. They provided agricultural brokering, banking, legal, mortuary, religious, and other needed services and drew into their circle frugal farmers who had been, or descended from, settlers. However, their interests were no longer the same as their grandfathers'. Small towns were a different culture in two ways. First, they contained massive numbers of new immigrants from Scandinavia and Germany who did not spread out into the land but clustered in communities. Second, they were increasingly prosperous. Now they were caught between two forces. One was a Jackson cycle that was increasingly irrelevant to them. The other was the rising industrialism that had nearly ruined them.

Ulysses S. Grant was the president who closed out this era. Regarded as ineffective, he had no idea how to deal with the financial crisis that hit toward the beginning of his second term, nor did he have any idea of how to deal with the transition that was coming. His standpoint derived from the Jackson era, which was always focused on land and modestly inflating currency. The problem was that the country consisted no longer of settlers clearing the land but of small towns (and because Grant was from Ohio, he should have understood that) and a surging industrialism that in about a quarter of a century would produce one-half of the world's manufactured products. There was an economic and social upheaval that could not be solved through the policies of the current cycle. But like all last presidents of a cycle, he had no other point of reference but the past. The social and economic cycle was about to turn again.

The Third Socioeconomic Cycle: The Hayes Cycle, 1876–1929

As with Jackson's election, the election of Rutherford B. Hayes was chaotic and full of charges and countercharges. The 1876 election is considered one of the dirtiest and most tumultuous in American history. Hayes received fewer votes than his opponent, Samuel Tilden, but won in the Electoral College. He won through complex chicanery that gave him the election. He was charged with stealing, which was not an irresponsible claim. However he was elected, Hayes presided over solving the problems left by the Civil War. Hayes, far from the icons Washington and Jackson were, repeated what they did. None of them created a new cycle, but they presided over it.

The economic crisis had to be solved because of the possibilities science was opening up and turning into technology. Two core technologies emerged during this period, both forms of energy, urgent if the Industrial Revolution was to proceed. The first was electricity, which spun off into a range of products from communications to illuminating the night. The second was the invention of the internal combustion engine, which radicalized transportation, particularly the automobile and aircraft, and created the oil industry. Industrialization was now transforming everyday life, and the appetite for new technologies created a hunger for capital.

The problem was that the financial crisis in 1873 still resonated, creating a capital shortage. Hayes and his Treasury secretary, John Sherman, a much more significant figure, chose to stabilize the currency but in a different way than Jackson had done. Jackson used silver as well as gold to back the dollar. Silver was more plentiful, both in citizens' hands and in the ground. Backing the currency with silver would have stabilized it without making it inflexible. Hayes's problem was a currency that had lost all confidence at a time when investment in industrialization was essential. Investors and bank depositors had to be certain that the value of their investment would not be undermined by runaway inflation.

Therefore, instead of using both gold and silver to back the dollar, Hayes chose to back it with only gold. A gold standard introduced rigidity, but it also instilled confidence. As the government repaid the war debt with gold-backed dollars, older gold-backed currency came back into circulation, no longer to be saved against impending collapse. This encouraged individuals to deposit their money into banks, and investment—including a great deal of foreign investment—began to flow rapidly into industrialization.

The introduction of a gold standard also tightened the money supply. In particular, it hit the poorer farmers who had trouble getting the credit they needed. Poorer farmers were being forced out, and wealthier farmers and small-town businessmen were able to acquire foreclosed farms at a discount. A substantial nostalgic movement arose that yearned for a return to the prewar era. William Jennings Bryan led an effort inside the Democratic Party for a return to a gold-and-silver-backed currency. His famed Cross of Gold speech in 1896 resonated, and he ran for president several times but couldn't win. Bryan was an advocate for the previous cycle, the one that had disappeared and was no longer relevant, even if he was still its powerful voice.

The small town, which had begun to emerge in the Jackson era, became the social foundation of this new era. It enforced moral behavior, including the most important virtues: frugality and hard work. In an age when investment capital was essential, hard work and frugality produced it. However, the small town was also the center of bigotry. It was a place of exclusion as well as intense community. The community worked, but it worked by imposing conformity through gossip and shaming. A small town is a dynamo that sustains life and wealth and can't live with disorder. Therefore, small towns excluded or confined in a subordinate place anyone who was different. They enforced the exclusion of African Americans, and Jews and Catholics were tolerated minimally. The distinction between the English and the Scots-Irish was gone. Germans and Scandinavians, who had begun arriving in large numbers before the Civil War, were accepted, although they tended to cluster in their own regions and towns. But Irish Catholics who had arrived at the same time were distrusted and tended to live in big cities.

The English had distrusted the Scots-Irish, and at first the farmers distrusted small-town merchants and bankers. Farmers lived through labor, whereas the small towns lived by trade. This was a crucial social distinction. It was also a cultural and moral difference. It was a normal process for the dominant class of the existing era to distrust the rising class and ethnicity of the forthcoming era. So those in small-town America deeply distrusted the large, flourishing industrial cities both for their sheer size and because they viewed the big cities as bastions of sin. In spite of the crowds, they reasoned, people were alone in big cities, and being alone, they were likely to fall more easily into sin. By contrast, they saw small towns as providing both community and morality.

People from small-town America also didn't like the people who lived in large cities, the wealthy and the masses of new immigrants arriving in the late nineteenth century. The cities were filled with Catholics from southern and eastern Europe, Jews, and African Americans who were beginning to migrate from the South, all with unknown loyalties, uncertain character, and none of the traits of Protestant small towns. The rising cities were seen as both alien and economically threatening, with industrialism taking the economic center from the commercial agriculture the small towns presided over.

The gold standard was generating massive investment. By 1900, the United States was producing half the manufactured goods in the world. For most of the third cycle, the United States was rapidly expanding its production and increasing its consumption. It constantly needed more labor, and immigrants swarmed in, enlarging the cities and making them even more exotic. The United States surged by every measure.

World War I set the stage for the problem that would force a cyclical shift. Massive industrial growth created a desperate need for customers. World War I destroyed customers. Loss of export markets placed pressure on American business, which was made up for by increased consumption driven by reduced tax rates. In 1929, the consumer bubble that had formed collapsed. But even before then, depression had hit the midwestern farm belt.

Many reasons are given to explain the massive industrial plant running out of customers, from excessive credit to Federal Reserve monetary policy. But it was impossible, given the global economic situation, to sustain the level of production that was constantly increasing between 1922 and 1927. Reflected in the irrational rise of the stock markets, a crisis was inevitable.

The crisis was not the crash of the markets. Rather, it was what resulted from the crash: a decline in employment and the decline of demand for manufactured products. As sales went down, employment went down. Therefore demand went down, and sales went down further, in a spiral that could not be arrested in the environment that Hayes had created. He had successfully propelled the American economy upward, but the same solutions that permitted the surge—a rigorous discipline imposed on the economy by the gold standard—could not solve the problem posed by the Depression.

Hayes had succeeded in generating massive investment through a stable currency. But the problem was that he had succeeded too well. The industrial plant of the United States outstripped the ability of the American and global markets to consume what it produced. Increasing savings would not address the problem. The solution was to increase consumption. But the strategy of the third era focused obsessively on encouraging investment. Encouraging consumption so as to utilize existing capacity was outside the framework of the era.

This era had been built around the gold standard and frugality. Industrialists had built the factories that enriched the country and sustained the elites. In creating the industrial system, they also undermined the system Hayes created. Factories produced goods at spectacular rates, but that production could only go forward if there were customers. The ideology of frugality, the interests of factory owners, and the availability of surplus labor via immigration inevitably suppressed wages. With wages stagnant and production increasing, the system went out of balance and finally, in 1929, went into a deep crisis.

Herbert Hoover was caught in a failed era. The assumption was that hard work and frugality would solve economic problems. Unemployment was viewed through the lens of the last era. It was assumed that unemployment was the result of the lack of work ethic of the jobless and if that was fixed they would go back to work. In the meantime, maintaining a balanced budget and restraining the money supply were the prudent things to do. The problem, of course, was that these two things reduced what wages there were, undermined demand, and left the economy in a worse condition. The model of the current era simply didn't work any longer. Herbert Hoover joined John Quincy Adams and Ulysses S. Grant as the final, failed president of an era.

The Fourth Socioeconomic Cycle: The Roosevelt Cycle, 1932–1980

The election of 1932 forced Hoover out and elected Franklin Roosevelt, who ran on a platform of frugality and a balanced budget. He actually had no clear plan, but he knew he couldn't do what

Hoover had done regardless of what he said to win the election. The problem was an absence of demand for the products being produced because workers were unemployed or had received pay cuts. The solution was anathema to that era: get money into the hands of the workers. Because they couldn't get jobs in bankrupt industries, the solution was to create jobs, even make-work jobs, in order to get money into their hands.

Intense political instability preceded the election. Throughout the 1920s, there was significant activity on the Left, including Communists, and anti-Communist activity by the federal government. The Ku Klux Klan had become increasingly powerful not only in the South but in the North as well. Huey Long, governor of Louisiana, appeared a viable candidate for president until his assassination in 1935. The close of the old cycle included the usual political dramatics.

The social foundation of this era was an urban industrial working class. That class comprised many migrants from Ireland and southern and eastern Europe, or their children and grandchildren, and southern whites who were struck by the Depression but actually had never recovered from the Civil War. They were either already organized or organizing into labor unions, which were allied with big-city Democratic machines. They demanded transfers of wealth. The Republicans were appalled. It didn't matter.

Roosevelt's policies were both necessary and insufficient. The imbalance between productive capacity and demand kept factories idle and workers unemployed. World War II finally ended the Depression. As we have seen, the industrial demands of World War II were overwhelming, and building a military dried up the workforce. The United States went from having a labor surplus to having a labor shortage. The war achieved what the New Deal intended to achieve. It eliminated unemployment and brought factories to full production.

The war introduced a period of prosperity built around a massive industrial plant that had been created for war and a highly skilled and disciplined workforce. The war also created a tremendous amount of pent-up demand, because civilian goods were in short supply or not being produced at all. What the war had achieved, in effect, was the Keynesian solution for depressions in an industrial society: substantial deficit spending. That resulted in a great deal of cash being placed in the hands of consumers who could not spend it during the war, and much of the cash was parked in war bonds. Demand was there; factories were there. One additional thing was needed.

One of the limiting and disciplining factors in prior eras had been the lack of consumer credit. Home mortgage lending was available in the early twentieth century, but it frequently required onerous terms. Credit for other goods was severely limited. The postwar era saw the increase not only in mortgages but in consumer credit for other products, such as automobiles. This evolved into credit for virtually everything via the credit card. The underlying principle was the founding principle of the cycle. Put factories to work by increasing demand. Jobs were one step. Consumer credit was the logical next step and the one that sustained the economy.

The Roosevelt era created the technology of management. The concept, taught at business schools and elsewhere, is neither hardware nor software. It is rather a method for thinking about an organization and controlling it. As mentioned previously, those who master this art are called technocrats. Technocrats are a class that is built around the principle of pragmatism. Getting the job done, whatever it is, is the art of the technocrat, and as they demonstrated in World War II, it was a powerful art. After World War II, they spread to manage not only business but government and other spheres of American life. The vast industries that had emerged during the Hayes era now came under the control of the technocrats.

Technocracy is a critical concept necessary to understand the last and next socioeconomic crisis. A technocrat is someone who has expertise in a certain area and credentials to certify that he has that expertise. In a way technocracy might simply be considered merit. The technocrat was someone who rose not because of his birth or because of his political acumen. He rose because he had the expertise needed to do his job, whatever that might be, in public or private life.

One of the critical aspects of the technocrat is that he had no ideology, or to put it another way, his only ideology was expertise—knowing something well. It was a class that spread to all areas, public or private, and carried with it the principle of efficiency. The technocrats represented a moral principle, however nonideological they wished to appear. That moral principle was the imperative toward efficiency in governance and all other spheres. It was therefore the expertise not of the plumber that was praised but of the manager, the professional, and the intellectual whose expertise was certified by the university. Thus, a class grew out of the relatively limited notion of the technocrat that arose in the Roosevelt era, a class that became powerful in the Reagan era.

The concepts of Roosevelt and Keynes worked extraordinarily well between 1945 and about 1970. It was a period of prosperity. In 1970, we saw the first indication of the termination of the cycle, when a relatively small wave of inflation hit and Richard Nixon put a wage and price freeze on the economy to stabilize it. Any slight possibility of this working disappeared in 1973, when the Arab countries placed an embargo on the sale of oil to the United States following the Arab-Israeli War. That action accelerated both inflation and the process of economic deterioration.

The solution to this depression became the next problem. The fourth era focused on high rates of consumption over investment. Further complicating this were high tax rates imposed on the upper income brackets. The tax rate on incomes over $250,000 was 70 percent. Wealthy investors, calculating risk, saw little reason to invest when success would cost 70 percent of the gain. Potential entrepreneurs were also discouraged from taking a risk where success was a long shot and the returns were severely capped.

As a result of the oil embargo, inflation surged. But underneath this problem was a deeper one. High demand had hidden an underlying problem with the industrial plant. It had aged, and the reluctance to invest curtailed the availability of capital to renew the industrial base. Countries like Germany and Japan, defeated in World War II, had many newer factories and produced more efficiently than American factories. They entered the U.S. market and took advantage of the credit-driven consumption.

The demand for money was high, both from consumers and from business. But the propensity to invest was low, which dramatically increased the cost of money. The natural impulse of this era was to try to increase consumption. The big problem with doing so was that U.S. factories were increasingly inefficient. Increasing demand drove up the purchases of foreign goods. In addition, increased utilization of inefficient plants meant falling profit margins; the more an inefficient plant is used, the higher the cost and the lower the profit.

All of this was preceded by massive political instability beginning twelve years before the defining election of 1980. In 1968, the Democrat leading the race for his party's nomination, Robert Kennedy, was murdered, along with Martin Luther King Jr. Massive riots broke out in Chicago during the Democratic National Convention. National guardsmen shot demonstrators at Kent State University in 1970. In 1974, Richard Nixon resigned after a wrenching crisis. As usual, the end of a cycle and the beginning of a new one were marked by political uncertainty, sometimes beginning more than a decade before the transition.

The result was the crisis of the 1970s, when inflation reached double digits, unemployment surged, and interest rates were astronomical. I bought my first home at a mortgage rate of 18 percent interest. Jimmy Carter had been elected president in 1976 and faced the full force of the capital shortage. His response, of course, was drawn from the Roosevelt era. That era opened on the Depression, and part of the solution to the Depression was to increase taxes on the investing class and put money into the hands of consumers. Carter followed the same plan. The problem he was facing was a shortage of capital and excessive demand forcing up prices and utilizing inefficient plants. What had made sense in the 1930s made little sense in the 1970s. Rather than improving the situation, it intensified the problem. Carter joined Hoover, Grant, and Adams in the role of presiding over the last phase of a cycle and doing what had once worked but did no longer.

The Fifth Socioeconomic Cycle: The Reagan Cycle, 1980–2030

The Reagan cycle solved the problem of capital shortage bequeathed to it by the Roosevelt cycle by shifting the tax structure. Reducing taxes on the upper, investor class freed up money for investment and also made taking the risk of investing more attractive. The result was a burst of investment in aging factories designed to modernize them and reengineer their management. Alongside this came a burst of entrepreneurial activity, heavily focused on the microchip. Investors, having had the rewards of success increased, were prepared to take risks. It was an expansion that would dominate the American, and global, economies until the 2008 financial crisis.

The Roosevelt cycle corporation, symbolized by General Motors, had been an efficient organization for much of that period. But its ability to grow declined. The internal combustion engine had reached a plateau in dramatic innovation, and the vehicle it powered had reached a plateau as well. By the mid-1950s, the automobile had reached a form that required minor technical evolution, not radical change. The emphasis was then on styling and marketing.

Competition grew and profit margins declined, and General

Motors searched for other ways to maintain growth. One was GMAC, the General Motors Acceptance Corporation, which began as a vehicle for financing auto purchases and evolved into an enormous financial institution. It generated more profits than vehicle sales did. The price of cars was capped by supply and demand, and the focus was on efficiency. Managers who knew relatively little about automobiles but a great deal about process took control of auto factories and tried to operate a range of businesses, from autos to finance. General Motors became so diffuse and entangled in so many industries that it could not compete in the core markets with Japanese and German companies, all of whom had much newer industrial plants and intense focus on their main product.

General Motors was an example of a corporation that had diffused, grown large and complex, and was therefore overstaffed. Many people were needed to maintain its complexity. Corporations like GM had to be reengineered because they had lost their core logic—return on capital, without which nothing else worked. Because such companies were so inefficient, countless longtime employees were let go. Many of those who were in their forties and fifties never found another job that paid at the same levels they'd been used to. Salaries and numbers were out of control. But it wasn't the employees' fault. It was the fault of a logic that led corporations to complexity and loss of focus.

The price of the increase of efficiency was a loss of jobs, particularly industrial jobs. But it was not the only price, because efficiency was created in two ways. One was organizational and technical; the other was in relocating factories to areas with lower costs, like China, or permitting exports from those countries. Both were designed to make the economy more efficient, but that resulted in needing fewer industrial workers.

At the same time, a revolution in the American economy was taking place. The microchip technology and a new wave of entrepreneurship combined to further disrupt the economy while creating a magnificent new economy and culture. The microchip transformed jobs. My father had been a typesetter in a printing factory. Type was set by hand at that time, and my father was a master craftsman. When computers were introduced into printing, his craftsmanship became obsolete, as was his job. He was one of millions who lost their jobs to a new technology at an age when they couldn't possibly learn the mysteries of the things that had replaced them. Sometimes their own company replaced them with new technology, but other times an entrepreneur destroyed the company they worked for or even destroyed an entire industry.

The theory of free trade is that it increases the wealth of nations. Left open are two questions. First, how long will it take to achieve this end? Second, how will the increased wealth be distributed? Free trade, and capitalism in general, are constantly creating new wealth and on the whole drive the economy forward. But "on the whole" excludes those who lose their jobs as the economic revolution takes place and never find a new job. In the abstract theory of the free market, this is a price that has to be paid. In the real world of society and politics, where the displaced have more power than they have in the economy, the reality is that this process can destabilize important and powerful sectors of the economy. That's what happened throughout the process, but it became a political reality in the middle of the second decade of the twenty-first century. The numbers grew and were concentrated in the same geographic areas.

The transformation had to happen. There was no way out of the Roosevelt cycle without the shifts made in the Reagan cycle. As in previous cycles, the problem was that the victims kept growing at the same time as the economy surged. Those who found new jobs started at the bottom of the escalator and found themselves tossed off time and time again. Median household income did not grow at all in fixed dollars.

Median household income in 2014 was about $53,000 with an average household size of 2.8 people. Income had hardly grown since 1975, a year in the middle of the last decade of the Roosevelt cycle. That gross income would come to about $3,400 in take-home pay a month, according to ADP payroll services.

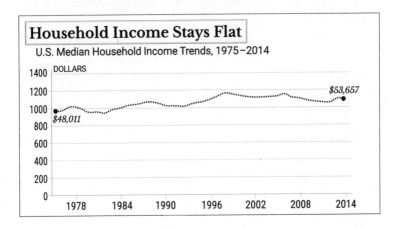

Household Income Stays Flat

U.S. Median Household Income Trends, 1975–2014

$48,011

$53,657

According to the Federal Reserve Bank of St. Louis, the median price of a home in the United States is $311,000. The monthly mortgage payment for a house of this price would be about $1,100, assuming the buyer put down 20 percent, or about $60,000, on the house. RealtyTrac.com puts the average tax per year on this home at 1.29 percent of total value, or $4,000 a year, $333 a month. Adding home insurance, the monthly cost of home ownership would be about $1,600, not counting maintenance. Almost half the money earned in the year would be spent on housing, leaving approximately $1,800 a month for all other expenses. Think of it as $450 a week for food, clothing, other debts such as car payments that average about $600 a month for a new low-cost car, and possibly student loans. And there are always unexpected expenses.

What we find is that the middle class currently can barely afford a middle-class life. Now think of the lower-middle class, which used to have a reasonably comfortable living as well. The current median income for the lower-middle class is about $30,000 annually. Take-home pay is about $26,000, or $2,166 a month. Spending half of the income on a mortgage, assuming the ability to come up with a down payment, would leave only $250 a week for all other needs, from car to food. It's not an option. The only option for the lower-middle class is an apartment, and a meager one at that.

Ironically, this deterioration occurred during one of the major booms in American history. GDP started growing faster than median household income in the early 1990s, and the gap widened throughout the rest of the Reagan cycle.

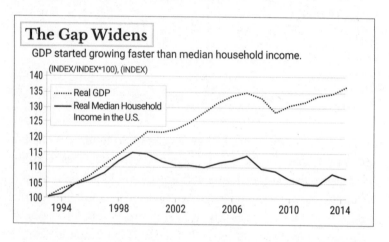

The Gap Widens

GDP started growing faster than median household income.

(INDEX/INDEX*100), (INDEX)

.... Real GDP

—— Real Median Household Income in the U.S.

GDP has increased by more than 35 percent since about 1993. Median household income has increased by a little over 5 percent during that time, but in real terms has declined since 1998. It was not the inequality that was important. Americans had always accepted inequality. It was the material standard of living that the middle class expected to enjoy that mattered to them. Owning a home and two cars and taking an annual vacation have been the definition of middle-class life and of the American dream. In the 1950s and 1960s, this was possible for the lower-middle class as well as the middle class. By the middle of the second decade of the twenty-first century, it was barely in the reach of someone with the median household income and not at all in the reach of the lower-middle class. It is a generalization but not an unreasonable one to say that this segment is the remnant of the white industrial working class, along with many other factions.

Total wealth had increased, but it flowed away from the industrial workers and toward those who worked in finance, technology, and other areas that now constitute the upper-middle class. But unlike before, it was not a smooth curve from lower-middle class to middle class to upper-middle class. There was a massive discontinuity between segments, the discontinuity in income between the old middle class and the new one.

The Reagan cycle succeeded so well that there is now a massive surplus of capital. Interest rates, which had been extremely high at the beginning of the cycle, plunged later. This was the result of a massive investment boom that generated substantial returns that, given tax rates, accumulated in the hands of investors. That accumulation, together with a decline in investment opportunities, drove the price of money down. Unfortunately, this does not make money easily accessible to small businesses. The financial crisis of 2008 resulted in extreme caution at any interest rate. Thus, there is a combination of limited money for small businesses and excess money chasing fewer investments as the microchip era matures.

Interest rates are now at historic lows. Vast amounts of money were generated at the start of the era, and most of it is in the hands of investment firms and individual investors, defined as people who have more money than they need to live. At the same time, as innovation has slowed, so has business formation. Opportunities to invest without large multiples have decreased, and those who invest in mature companies face the challenge of an increasingly risky environment, as usually exists at the end of an era.

There is a great deal of money searching for and not finding investment opportunities. The cash is being held in very safe assets, depressing interest rates dramatically. Even retirees who have planned their finances with care did not expect to be getting almost no interest for their wealth. The dislocation of industrial workers, coupled with the damage done to prudent savers by low interest rates, has begun to generate an economic crisis. Inevitably, there follows a social crisis.

The new economic crisis flows from the very success of the Reagan cycle, which generated a great deal of wealth but distributed it in the end, as it did in the beginning, with a focus on increasing money for investment. But as with all cycles, the problem solved in the current cycle generates the problem to solve in the next. The social problem that flows from this economic crisis is the tension between the declining class, the industrial working class, and the coalition that has in some way benefited from the rise of what we might call the technological class—entrepreneurs and investors. And with the social crisis, a cultural crisis must arise. That cultural crisis is in many ways the cutting edge of the others, because in pitting rising and falling classes against each other, the struggle may be economic, but the driving edge is a divergence in values.

We can see when we look at each of these five cycles how interconnected the social and cultural changes are to the economy. As an example, the technocracy's increasing control of American life was made possible by abundant consumer credit after World War II and the emergence of a new social class: the suburbanite. The suburbanites' needs drove industrial, governmental, educational, medical, and all other spheres, managed by technocrats. The postwar generation could buy homes, as well as furniture, cars, or trips, and pay for them on anticipated income. From the point of view of the prior era, this was the height of irresponsibility and even immorality. From the standpoint of the well-to-do, suburbia was poorly constructed housing without culture or a soul. The urbanites looked at the suburbs as they had been looked at by small-town America. Small-town America saw the urbanites as the essence of irresponsibility. New social forms are always held in contempt by those in previous eras. But the technocrats, who were created along with the suburbs, understood that their task was to serve the emerging reality.

In laying out these five economic cycles, I have tried to show the broad cycles that have forced the evolution of the United States. But another point is that these cycles work in similar ways. The prior cycle reaches a failure point, or perhaps more precisely becomes increasingly inefficient. Before that failure becomes fully apparent, political crises break out, starting as much as a decade before the crisis demands a solution. The political is the seismograph of emerging social and economic earthquakes. New social forces emerge and mature, dividing the country in new ways. The economy enters a period in which economic dysfunction becomes unbearable to one social faction, even while another continues to benefit. The old social order had contempt for the new one, and vice versa, and that contempt intensifies the political problem while retarding needed economic changes. The old social order believes that the future should be a continuation of the past. The new social order demands a radically different approach. Roosevelt was held in contempt by the old elite, which also dismissed the new social class, while the newly emerging social force had contempt for the anti-Roosevelt old-money elites and small-town America. They in turn had contempt for the urban industrial workers who were challenging them.

It is always a time of tension and mutual loathing that appears to be tearing the country apart. The last act of the decaying era is the election of a president utterly committed to the principles and practices of the prior era. These presidents—Adams, Grant, Hoover, and Carter—brought the crisis to a head by intensifying the crisis by taking obsolete measures in an effort to solve the problems they faced. After this presidency, a new president is elected who, because of either understanding or simply reacting to reality, dramatically shifts the economic policies of the old era and, having been elected by the emerging social faction, begins the extended process of cycling in a new era.

That is the process that we are living through at the moment. The Reagan era has reached its limits and can't sustain the economy. The failure is in the process of creating a new set of competing social classes. This is reflected in the intensifying political crisis of the Trump presidency, in which the new social forces begin battling each other. This crisis will last through to the 2020s. In 2024, a new president will emerge who represents the values of the declining era. The failure of his presidency will bring to power the rising class who will impose a new economic orthodoxy.

And finally, in the 2030s (following the storms that began in 2016), a new cycle will emerge. Over the following few years in the 2030s, the political confrontation, social tension, and economic dysfunction will be solved. The cycle will have created a new era, different from the past but built on the same foundation of invention, and it will endure for another half a century.

PART THREE

THE CRISIS AND THE CALM

8

First Tremors of the
Coming Storm

When Donald Trump emerged as the winner of the American presidency, I was in Australia. The announcement came shortly before noon, and I spent the day—and the visit—being asked in various conferences and by perplexed media hosts how Trump could have won and what it would mean. The election was taken as seriously in Brisbane and Sydney as it was in Cincinnati or New York. Already working on this book, I tried to explain that the focus should be not on the man but on his place in the cycle. It did not go over well, because the fascination was with his personality. That remains the case, but I will argue that that is a mistake.

Donald Trump's election in fact signaled the beginning of the lead-up to the fourth institutional cycle and to the sixth economic and social cycle. The current institutional model has been increasingly unable to function successfully, and the key lies in redefining the relationship of the federal government to itself. The economic and social crises have created a massive decline in the condition of what had previously been a pillar of American society: the industrial workers. Because there has never been a period when both cycles reached their crises almost simultaneously, we can expect the 2020s to be an exceptionally unstable time. The lead-up to the 2020s has started that way, with an election in 2016 in which each candidate clearly represented a segment of society that was at odds with the other. And the election ended in a virtual tie, with Hillary Clinton winning the popular vote, and Trump the Electoral College vote. That, more than anything, indicated how tense a time it would be.

The 2016 election signaled that the political system had sensed the underlying tension, just as happened in the 1968 elections. The political conflict of 1968 would not be closed until 1980. So too the political tensions of 2016 won't be closed until 2028. First recall that there has always been a politician from the declining class who holds the final presidency in a cycle and oversees a failed presidency. This will likely be a Democrat standing for the technocracy—a conventional Democrat in the sense that Jimmy Carter was a conventional Democrat, Herbert Hoover was a conventional Republican, and so on. Such terminal presidents, with the exception of Ulysses S. Grant, are one-term presidents. So I will surmise that the final president of this cycle will be elected in 2024 (or in 2020 if he is a two-term president).

As cycles come to an end, the first indication is the emergence of political instability that can begin more than a decade before the shift to a new cycle. For example, the shift to the Reagan cycle began with political instability during the late 1960s. But the political instability gave no hint as to what the new cycle would look like. The antiwar movement or the resignation of Richard Nixon provided no hint of the nature of the new cycle, whose beginning was presided over by Ronald Reagan. The political system is sensitive and rapidly transmits the tremors of even small economic and social shifts. The economic and social difficulties that would emerge intensely in the 1970s were beginning to assert themselves, out of sight to most observers but already destabilizing the political system. Thus, political instability is the preface to a social and economic crisis that perhaps a decade later will become unsustainable. The old cycle collapses under its own weight, to be replaced by a new cycle, symbolized by a new president. Reagan did not create the new cycle. He exploited the intense tensions of the dying cycle to become president and then presided over the birth of the new one. Had it not been Reagan, it would have been someone else, but the old was gone and the shape of the new had been set by the restless instability of the old.

Donald Trump's election was the first indication that the Reagan cycle is coming to an end. The election was extremely contentious, each side vilified the other, and the side that lost insisted that they had been robbed. It was contentious because fundamental shifts are taking place in American society. The side that was experiencing the pain of change saw the other side as the agents of their misery. The side that was not experiencing it saw the other side as "deplorable," to use Hillary Clinton's phrase. They were deplorable because they clung to a culture that was seen as outmoded and wicked. All this was further complicated by the fact that the winner of the election lost the popular vote and won only through the Electoral College vote. This led Trump's enemies to regard his presidency as illegitimate, while Trump's supporters claimed that illegal immigrants stole his popular majority.

The political tension did not dissipate with the election but mounted astronomically after it. Each side of the political divide hurled vile insults at the other, with each side convinced that the other was dangerous and irresponsible. The focus was on personalities; Trump, his opponents, and the issues were submerged into the vast distrust that engulfed the country. Perhaps most important was the fact that the factions were so deeply divided that in many cases no one knew anyone who disagreed with them and friendships between those who were political opponents were hard to find. It was really not the loathing of Trump or Clinton that was driving the discord; that was merely a symptom. The true problem was the division within the country, which was struggling mightily with real social, economic, and institutional dysfunction that drove the tensions.

It was the kind of election we would expect as we begin to enter the transition phase. Remember the chaos that began in 1968, or read about the charges and countercharges between Hayes and Tilden in 1876 or between Adams and Jackson in the 1824 election. As the economy begins to shift, the social structure shifts as well. Inevitably, pain starts to course through at least part of the system. The result is the start of political turmoil that is frightening and appears insoluble. Many see it as a sign that the country is coming apart, but in truth it is simply evidence of a rapidly evolving country passing through an orderly change.

Each cyclical change involves intense incivility between the clashing social forces. That is not a new phenomenon by any means. In the 1960s, it was the antiwar/antiestablishment faction against Middle America. In some sense, both of these factions were fictional, because they had endless schisms within them. But they shared a common loathing. One movement condemned the brutal and plastic inauthenticity of the other. The other movement condemned the traitorous and licentious principles of the other. The precise invective is immaterial, and none of it was still there in 1980. It was not the terms of mutual disgust that mattered, but the intensity and the division of the country into what appeared to be two incompatible factions.

It is interesting to note that at the time of political instability there is frequently a new communication technology that is blamed for the dissemination of negativity or vitriol. In the 1960s, it was television, rendering the country passive victims of the news media. In the 1920s, it was the movies, peddling a form of collective sentimentality and licentiousness, along with radio introducing the immediacy of news. There is always a new form of media that is blamed, but these media are just ways to explain the unexpected rancor of the time. The Internet allows millions to read, and social media allows people to voice their views in unprecedented ways, but the users of the Internet and social media fall into tribes. They follow others who are peddling ideas they already agree with and intensify existing feelings. The tribalism of the Internet actually limits the penetration, just as FOX is followed by its partisans and MSNBC by its.

This division and rancor are not new. As the social and economic cycles shift, division and rancor are always there. Before Reagan, the country split between the counterculture and Middle America. Before Roosevelt, there was the Red Scare, the populism of Huey Long, and the confrontation between the urban ethnic immigrants, on the one hand, and small-town America and the rich on the other. Before Hayes, there was the Civil War, and so on. Rancor is not new, nor is it new to blame a new communication mode. During a transition process, particularly the first phase, the sense of public anger is magnified, usually tied to emerging economic and social pain.

We are currently seeing something slightly different. What makes this transition between cycles unique is not the Internet or the tension but, as I have said, the fact that both the socioeconomic cycle and the institutional cycle will reach crisis points at about the same time. There has been one transition that came close (approximately fifteen years apart), which was the social and economic crises that struck in 1929 in the form of the Great Depression and the institutional transition that took place in 1945 at the end of World War II. But cycles always end in failure, and now for the first time both cycles will be failing simultaneously. Either cycle's failure places stress on the political system. In this case, there will be unprecedented stress, and we are feeling it already—the outer winds of the coming storm.

The two cycles have become intertwined. The socioeconomic cycle has created a social and political reality that deeply divides the country in terms of wealth and in terms of culture. The Rust Belt is still starving for jobs, and American industry has moved on. The very term "Rust Belt" explains what happened. The auto industry, once the engine driving the American economy, is a shadow of its past.

The new engine, business built on the microchip, enriches Boston or San Francisco, leaving the auto assembly lines to rust. Many have benefited from this; others have been devastated. Tension is deep and inevitable and stretches beyond economics to deep cultural disagreements, between a class rooted in traditional institutions and a class leaving tradition behind. There is nothing new in this progression. The debate was once over the right of women to vote. This time it is about lifestyles like homosexual marriage. One cycle ends and another begins, and in between there is mutual contempt and rage.

The institutional crisis is seen in a federal government that has both dissipated its attention and fragmented its structure. The federal government is doing so much and is divided into so many parts that creating a coherent military strategy or a comprehensible health-care reform bill becomes impossible. It is a structure that can no longer focus on the problem or conceive of the solution. Nor are the elected representatives, the president and Congress, capable of controlling a system so diffused and fragmented. As this old institutional cycle comes to an end, as others have, organization and reality diverge.

The problem of the first institutional cycle was that it was unclear whether the federal government was sovereign over the state. The matter was settled in the Civil War. The problem of the second institutional cycle was that a sovereign federal government had limited authority over the economy and society. As I have shown, this was settled in World War II. The problem of the third institutional cycle is that the door was opened for massive federal oversight of American life, without defining limits and without establishing an institutional structure capable of managing its vast authority.

Public dissatisfaction with the federal government has always been part of American life. An old joke was that the biggest lie was saying, "I'm from the government and I'm here to help." But the situation has changed significantly in 2019 as opposed to the twentieth century. During World War II, the president, as commander in chief, took control of much of the American economy and society. The Cold War followed, and while the tide of power receded, the principle emerged that the president was no longer just one of three equal branches. In the execution of foreign policy, he became the primary force. In the management of society, he was less elevated, but the executive branch had enormous power in interpreting laws and turning them into regulations. The power of the government made it essential to have a powerful executive, and the power of the executive created an institutional imbalance.

This new vastness of federal power over society required not only a strong president. Even more, it required a vast administrative structure. President Obama's health-care act was around 897 documents with over twenty thousand pages of regulations to explain it. Compare this with the original Social Security law, which was twenty-nine pages long. The Social Security Act has now grown to twenty-six hundred pages, and the regulations are vast as well. Effective power (as opposed to elected, or intended, power) was passed to a vast army of managers and civil servants who defined the regulations, and therefore could redefine the intent of Congress, not intentionally, but simply because no one person could comprehend the whole. Making the regulations consistent with the law, and even with themselves, became impossible.

For most people, particularly those like the poor or the disabled, who are most dependent on the federal government for a range of needs, the federal government is incomprehensible, and the ability to petition the government, a constitutional right, is irrelevant in practice. For others—for example, technology professionals—the federal government has minimal implications for their lives. For the wealthy, navigating the federal regulations that impact them requires large numbers of lawyers and accountants, specialists in federal regulation—an expense that is simply the cost of business. In a democratic society, being unable to petition or understand the federal government—except if one has the ability to maintain a staff of professionals—creates an inherent distrust of government. The class of Americans who supported the rise of the federal government after World War II found themselves incapable of understanding the complexity of the system, nor able to afford counsel. They found themselves the object that was administered rather than a citizen served.

In a way, all of this was summed up in the wars fought after September 11. The president overwhelmingly controlled those wars, and yet his ability to create a goal that could be reached, or define a means of achieving it, became impossible. Even so, our troops remained engaged. This process has been visible since Vietnam and is now intensifying. The president surrounds himself with experts, with the cabinet no longer playing the role of chief advisers, and Congress acts more or less as an onlooker. The experts are focused on the issue at hand rather than on the broader question of American interests. Or more precisely, they confuse the area in which they are experts with the area the United States should focus on. As with domestic matters, the public loses not just control but also an understanding of what is going on, and under the presidential power of secrecy the confusion is institutionalized.

The result is a massive mistrust of the federal government by those who need it the most and can understand it the least, not because they are not smart enough to understand it but because the federal government has become institutionally opaque as well as not fully coherent in its actions. The vastness of its authority overwhelms the system's ability to coordinate and focus and shifts authority from the constitutional division of powers to those formally in the executive branch.

Donald Trump won the election by grasping the alienation of broad sectors of society, not only from the federal government, but also from those who serve in it. There was a collision between the federal technocracy and those who had experienced and distrusted it. And Trump faced a party organized around Hillary Clinton, who was the quintessential advocate of federal power and technocracy. The election determined nothing more than that the crisis of distrust was beginning.

The economic and social issue had started to show itself. The Reagan era had kicked off a wave of innovation and created a powerful class of entrepreneurs and technologists. Left behind were the masses who had been employed in classical industrialism in which the financial community could no longer invest, given foreign competition. Two core classes had emerged, and they had very different interests and very different lives. This was the other side. Obviously, the classes were far more complex and varied than technologists versus industrialists, and many individuals on both sides match the profile. But still, at the core this was the distinction.

And the social and economic division matched and reinforced the institutional dilemma. Technocracy had come to dominate both the institutional and the socioeconomic cycles. Technocracy is a simple concept. It believes that problems should be solved through knowledge and that problem solving of all sorts is technical in nature. Technology is not just a machine but a mode of approaching a problem. A civil servant in Washington working on health care is using a rational, methodical, and therefore technical approach to a problem, in the same sense that someone designing a microchip is doing.

As I discussed previously, technocracy was built on the concept of nonideological solutions for government. Yet technocracy has now developed into an ideology in itself. Its vision of the world is that it is understandable and can be perfected by those who have the knowledge to understand and manipulate the world. And it follows from this assumption that these people should be permitted to manage the system. The technocrat may serve the interests of the public, and he not only helps define those interests but also needs control of the machinery of social organizations like government, business, universities, and prisons, in order that his technical expertise can be brought to bear. It is a class of credentials and achievement, of MBAs and computer scientists and masters in public policy, with a powerful smattering of entrepreneurs whose success is their credentials. The technocrats saw expertise as the only measure of a person. Therefore, distinctions of race, gender, sexuality, or citizenship were of no importance. Part of their political program was to ensure that such characteristics did not hinder anyone's ability to become an expert.

We need to understand the breadth of technocracy. Whether a civil servant, a Hollywood producer, a book editor, a financial engineer, or a college professor, there is belief in the power of the mind to shape the world. The technocracy emerges from the Enlightenment, and as such it believes that reason can perfect the world or, if not perfect it, vastly improve it. What needs to be improved is the status of the oppressed, both in the United States and in the world as a whole. When technocrats move beyond their own area of expertise, they share a view of the world that is not equal (the financial inequality of the technocracy itself is massive) so much as freed from oppression. But technocracy does believe, above all, that someone must be judged on expertise and knowledge and not on incidental characteristics. To do so is oppression.

But what is their definition of the oppressed? It is not the economically oppressed that they have come to defend but the culturally oppressed. African Americans, regardless of their economic status, suffer from the effects of racism. Hispanics suffer from xenophobia, as do Muslims. Those who deviate from the sexual norm are the victims of homophobia. Women are the victims of misogyny. Racism, xenophobia, homophobia, and misogyny are all defects in the victimizer. Therefore, they believe, it is the victimizer who must be constrained and reformed, by reshaping his thinking and punishing those who cannot abandon the thoughts of oppression.

Technocrats live their lives abstractly, even while they are managing their own sphere. For them, all problems are intellectual. You must think constantly, and that thinking makes action possible. Once you have thought, the doing simply follows. Reason leads to language, and the battleground of the technocrat is language. If the language is reshaped, so will be the action. Political correctness, as it's called, is the manner in which the technocrats as the ascendant class reshaped the world. The tension of the technocracy is between their work in their own fields and the universal principles that they practice.

This shows itself most clearly in the way they deal with the declining class, the heavily white, industrial working class. In the thinking of the technocracy, the fundamental cause of oppression is whites who have historically oppressed using race, nationality, and gender. But the technocrats draw a sharp distinction between themselves (predominantly white) who are at least engaged in a struggle to transcend oppression in thought and speech and those whites who continue to practice it. This declining class is plunging economically, but for the technocracy, which embraces a vast range of incomes, that decline is not of the essence. It is their unwillingness to abandon oppression.

The industrial working class is older. Its decline began some forty years ago. Their children have also suffered from the decline but need to be thought of differently. The parents' lives were shaped by what they could do with their hands. Their world was physical, a world of machines and of physical nature that had to be subdued. Their pride was in their physical strength and in their common sense. "Common sense" is a complex term, but it boils down to knowledge of the world, as they know it, and the things that are common to us all, at that time and in that place. The goals of the industrial working class were not to change the world but to find a secure place in it, to understand its rules and to live within them.

The white working class exists in a world of received, not constructed, morality. The morality they received was learned from their parents and their churches. By the 1980s, the majority of the white working class was Catholic and Protestant, many from conservative denominations. They regarded homosexuality, premarital sex, gay marriage, and abortion as inherently immoral. As with all people, what they believed to be moral and what they actually did were often different things.

Members of this class find themselves now in a world where their churches' views, the most authoritative imaginable, are considered not only wrong but a form of phobia. Those churches remain to them both legitimate and enormously powerful, and their churches are under attack. The attacks don't weaken their morality but in fact harden it into a sense of embattlement. Something that was ingrained from such a powerful authority, when attacked, will inevitably result in a counterattack, and that counterattack comes in political terms.

Racism has always been part of American history, but the issue now is not so much racism in the mind of the white working class as a matter of selective injustice. They resent that there are special programs for "oppressed minorities" but no one seems to care that white working-class incomes are in decline and birth rates of unwed mothers of this class now approach 50 percent. Drug use has become a vast epidemic. In other words, the condition of the white working class now is not dissimilar to the condition of African Americans in the 1970s.

The condition of African Americans became a matter of overriding national concern, spawning programs, the most controversial of which was affirmative action. The technocracy attempted, however poorly, to address the condition of the collapsing African American family. No such concern is forthcoming from the technocracy today concerning the white working class. Rather, the technocrats regard them as being the problem, while the white working class see themselves as being just as deserving as African Americans or Hispanics. Their point is that they as a class were hurt and forgotten by the post-Reagan era and really not until Trump did they have someone who finally understood and would speak out for them.

The technocracy has the upper hand against the white working class, although it is a tenuous hand, as can be seen by the election of Donald Trump. But this is merely the opening confrontation. Pressure on the technocracy will build. America is heading toward an institutional crisis in which the competence of the technocracy and the institutions of the federal government will be questioned. Pressure from one direction will come from the broader geopolitical crisis, and the growing inability of the technocracy to define an institutional solution for America as an empire. In the same sense, the ability of the technocracy to create coherent solutions to social problems is severely limited, partly as a result of its ideology, partly because of its failure to simplify complex problems.

The white working class was not unanimous in support of Trump, nor was it alone in supporting him. But while no class was as supportive of Trump as the white working class, many fragments of other classes supported him. Hillary Clinton, as I have said, was the candidate of the technocracy. She ran for office based on her credentials and vociferously spoke for the oppressed. She won the popular vote but lost the election because that vote was heavily concentrated in the Northeast and on the West Coast. In other words, she won the heartland of the technocracy and lost the heartland of the country—the declining industrial base. The election showed that we had reached gridlock between the two major competing classes. It was not the industrial working class that defeated Clinton but the geographic concentration of her support and defection of voters that ought to have voted for her.

One dimension explaining Hillary Clinton's loss was Libya. In spite of the failure of U.S. strategy in Afghanistan and Iraq, the United States chose to conduct air attacks to depose a tyrant, Muammar Gadhafi. Gadhafi was killed, but chaos was unleashed, including the death of the U.S. ambassador to Libya. Leaving aside all the other issues associated with this, the decision to depose another dictator flew in the face of what had been learned in Iraq, or as a consequence of a rising in Syria. This was intended as a humanitarian intervention, and the technocracy in the State Department saw this as a morally necessary intervention that carried with it little risk. Clinton was hammered on other aspects of Libya, but it was the incoherence of the policy that hurt her the most. Every time she praised her foreign policy experience, Libya came up.

Clinton's Libya problem encapsulated the weak point of the technocracy. The argument for expertise as the basis for political authority depends on the experts' success at managing both their small niche and society as a whole. In a sense, this is the justification for any class's authority, but it is unique and radical to the technocrats. If they fail, their claim to authority and their justification to rule dissolve. When the technocrats become a ruling faction, they have a unique requirement to do well. Because governance and expertise have a relationship, but a far more distant one than might be imagined, the more they move into the business of governing, the less their expertise matters.

Andrew Jackson claimed the right to govern not because he was the smartest man in the room. He based it on his bravery and cunning. Being the smartest man in the room leaves anyone vulnerable. Things are expected of him that he cannot deliver, because intelligence by itself is insufficient to govern. In a society based on knowledge, it would seem obvious that those with knowledge would be the natural rulers. Things are not as simple as that. The technocrats laid claim to acquired knowledge. Those who argued for common sense and their notion of morality opposed them.

Economic interest and culture have been clashing since the Bush administration. It was a mild clash, because the Republican and Democratic Parties essentially affirmed the economic system as it was, and that in the end was the core issue. The Republicans did tend to stand in opposition to the dominant culture over matters of sexual mores and did tend to raise questions about the institutional functionality of the federal government, but the latter was pro forma, and the former was primarily to hold the more traditional-leaning segment of its coalition in the party.

Under Barack Obama, the challenge to the economic model became more intense, with the emergence of the Tea Party. And with the emergence, there was more intense questioning of the right of the federal government to intrude on society both on ideological and on practical grounds. At the same time, the Democrats became more dogmatic on the economic principles and the ideological and cultural issues. The two parties began to drift apart. However, the mainstream of the Republican Party, the sector where presidential candidates were spawned, remained intact.

But underneath the surface, the economic situation was intensifying. The year 2008 was the breaking point, where the impact of the subprime crisis hit the declining class more directly than the technocracy. As important, it appeared to the white industrial class that the federal government was committed to protecting the interest of all classes but theirs, while the ability of the federal government to function at all was declining.

The white industrial class believed that both the technocracy and the federal government had turned against them, their economic problems, and their cultural values and ideology. The technocrats were doing relatively well economically. Their moral principles were making inroads, and the general ideology they propounded was dominant. From the point of view of the declining class, both political parties were indifferent if not opposed, in varying degrees, to their interests.

Albeit declining economically and socially, the white industrial class was still vast, disorganized but holding common principles. They were going to be able to force the issue, particularly in the Republican Party, where the weakness of the power structure was revealed by the Tea Party. If they became organized, they would become an irresistible force in the party. Inevitably, someone would come along to organize them, but it had to be someone outside the party, someone not trapped in the web of relationships that accepted the basic economic and social model.

The leader was less important than the sentiment that had formed. He simply had to recognize it was there and speak to it. None of the other Republicans could do that. They could not reject basic principles such as free trade and respect for immigrants. What the rest of the Republican Party didn't realize is that what had been a marginal trend in the Republican Party had now become dominant. Failing to understand that, they could not speak to this class.

Donald Trump promised to make America great again. This made no sense to the rest of the party or to the technocracy, both of whom believed that America not only had retained its greatness but was enhancing it. For the members of the declining industrial class, America was, in fact, in decline because their own position was becoming increasingly tenuous. Trump insulted, promised, raged; he did everything a good politician would never do. But that was precisely his strong point. He did not speak like a conventional politician. What the rest of the Republican field failed to understand was the degree to which the conventional politician was by this point held in contempt.

Trump was incomprehensible to the technocrats because the white industrial class was incomprehensible to them. In the same way that the Democrats could not fathom Ronald Reagan's victory or the Republicans Franklin Roosevelt's, Trump was incomprehensible. The focus was on Trump, his peculiarities, and his outrageous comments. But that was not the issue, any more than Hillary Clinton's server was the issue. Clinton acted as if her position were already won because Trump was self-evidently unacceptable and because the people who supported him were considered marginal, the "illness" that had to be cured.

They were not marginal, nor were they in control. The 2016

election was essentially a tie resulting in a noisy gridlock. Trump was locked in institutionally and locked in by his nongovernmental opposition, particularly the media. He could not convert his opponents, nor could his opponents convert his supporters.

Therefore, Trump does not represent the transition to the new era. He is instead the first tremor who appeared decisive to his supporters and frightening to his opponents. Trump is the first indicator of a struggle between two classes. But while the ascending class has not yet reached its limit, the descending class is continually bleeding power. That means that the 2020s will be more complex than even the current configuration hints at.

9

The Crisis of the 2020s—
a Clashing of Cycles

The first political tremors have been felt, the anger has mounted, and the sides have been arrayed against each other. The preface to the tale has been written, but oddly, as the underlying institutional, social, economic, and geopolitical problems emerge into full view, the rage shifts away from the political, and the nation begins to entertain the possibility that the American project has failed. There was a great deal of discussion like this in the 1970s, which led Jimmy Carter to make a famous speech called by the press the "malaise speech," where he discussed the American "crisis of confidence." Similarly, in the 1930s as the social and economic stresses sapped the nation's morale, Roosevelt said, "The only thing we have to fear is fear itself." There is much discussion today, but even as we await the next election, we must realize that we are on the doorstep of the real crisis and not yet in the crisis itself.

Socioeconomic cycles are shaped by social and economic failure. Institutional crises are shaped by the wars the United States has been fighting. In the 2020s, the two major cycles that have shaped the United States will intertwine, and the sense of failure will be deep, even as the solution to the economic and social problems will be grinding through the system. The political system will become less significant as the problems appear to be overwhelming it. It is difficult to be politically passionate when being increasingly cynical—not only about politicians, a traditional American stance, but about the system as a whole. Political passion rests on believing that it matters. In the 2020s, regardless of whether President Trump is reelected, indifference coupled with cynicism will dominate. The crisis of this decade will spring from very real problems but will also be a crisis of faith in the Republic itself.

When we talk about history, the tale is filled with people and events. Such a history has value, but it also misses the point. When we think about the last decade, filled with Donald Trump and Vladimir Putin, China and Ukraine, we are discussing the tip of the iceberg. The real story is told by the rest of the iceberg, the deep structure and its development that is difficult to see but that controls the actors and events.

Let's begin with the institutional cycle. The first cycle created the federal government, the second redefined the relationship of the federal government to the states, the third cycle redefined the federal government's relation to the economy and society, and the fourth cycle will redefine the relationship of the federal government to itself. By this I mean redefine how the federal government sets priorities, how it focuses on achieving the priorities, and how it is held accountable. This sounds like a relatively minor shift. It is, in fact, as radical as the shift after World War II. The shift will transform a massive entity that is entangled with all aspects of society, and in doing so, it will change not only those relationships but how society itself works.

In the third and current cycle, the federal government divided into two elements. There were the elected officials, as well as their direct subordinates, and the unelected managers. It's been this way since the beginning of the United States, but the balance between the two shifted in the third cycle, with the managers becoming more autonomous and entwined with all aspects of government, as well as many parts of society. Formally, this shift happened outside the bounds of politics (in that it did not involve itself in electoral politics), but it had a subtle political ideology, which was the ideology of expertise.

This ideology is rooted in the nature of the institutional crisis, supported to some degree by the socioeconomic crisis. As we have seen increasingly in the past several decades, the foundation of the institutional problem was the vast expansion of the authority of the federal government, and apparent power, and its inability to create coherent and understandable laws and policies. By understandable, I mean the ability of citizens subject to these laws to understand them. An example that I will mention often is the Affordable Care Act, which affects virtually everyone's life yet is so long and complex that hardly anyone has a comprehensive understanding of its meaning.

Expansion in the mission of the federal government has created a belief in its effective power. Its ineffectiveness is therefore seen not as a systemic failure but as the result of a deliberate failure designed to benefit the powerful and harm the many. In other words, because the power of the federal government isn't doubted, its failures are perceived by an increasing number of people as deliberate. Therefore, as in all social fears, there will be an increasing belief in the coming decade that the federal government is in the hands of conspirators. Such a conspiracy was unthinkable in the two prior institutional cycles, because federal power was simply not that vast. But in the 2020s the image of the federal government will make deliberate collusion the only coherent explanation for its failure. This distrust will feed into the fear of economic interests generated by the socioeconomic cycle's failure.

Psychologically, the decade of the 2020s will be a grim time, with the real institutional, social, economic, and geopolitical failures being ignored. It is a frightening thought to think that unseen forces are in control of the nation. It is even more frightening, perhaps, to face the truth, which is that no person is really in control and that the institutions are. The federal system has been built, since World War II, on the assumption of expertise, and for a good part of that time it functioned effectively. But accepting the idea that expertise can result in failure will require a stunning shift in the public's perspective, even though holding the government in contempt has long been part of the culture. This is a key threat to the institutional structure of the third cycle and the technocracy that controls the institutions. The pressure of the U.S. global role and the inability of the technocracy to break out of the intellectual gridlock it finds itself in will be the two most important factors in the shifting institutional cycle of the 2020s.

The source of the problem is the idea that because expertise is essential, it should govern. Government by experts (the meaning of technocracy) consists mostly of experts approaching problems through their own prisms, hoping that the many prisms created can be brought together in a single whole and comprehended by the public. That is an essential part of democratic life. However, it rarely happens because the person who understands the public, the person who tries to consolidate the myriad parts, and the experts who craft the solution all find each other incomprehensible. The result is, by default, government by experts. It is a government of vast responsibility and vast knowledge that is bogged down in its own complexity, with serious consequences for the nation.

Consider foreign policy, an area that is the central responsibility of the federal government. As we have seen, the three prior institutional cycles emerged from war. The fourth one is now starting to emerge from both a war and a massive geopolitical shift. The war is the one that began on September 11, 2001. But the critical thing to remember is that since 2001 the United States has been in a constant state of war, even if not on the scale of World War II or the Civil War. But it is a war that has lasted far longer than any other in American history. And in the inability of the government to frame the war in such a way that it might be won, the institutions of the United States revealed their fundamental weaknesses. War requires a simplification, an understanding of a desired end, clarity on strategy, and allocation of resources appropriate to both. The government proved incapable of the clarity needed for a war because it could not simplify. The complexity of the government was translated into a complicated plan for the war, and the complexity trapped the warriors in a confusion that undermined their mission.

But there was a deeper issue. In December 1991 the Soviet Union collapsed. The United States found itself in a position it had never anticipated and in which it did not want to be. The United States had not only become the sole global power; it had also become an empire, a nation that influenced and impacted virtually all other nations. What will the United States do with the empire it has become? Many people have denied this obvious fact, and others want to get rid of it. Still others want to create liberal democracies throughout the world. Some feel that the State Department is a superb instrument of power. Others despise it. The argument is intense, but there is a general feeling that something is terribly wrong with the federal government, and we can expect that perception to intensify in the 2020s. As I have explained, the problem of managing foreign policy is what normally shifts institutions. World War II was an industrial war, and U.S. industry had to be mobilized to manage it. Therefore, purely business-oriented considerations and leaders had to be controlled by managers answerable to the state. The consequences of the rise of America as the dominant global power and eighteen years of war in the Middle East will force the World War II–type institutions in which power is concentrated in Washington to be replaced. The federal government wasn't designed by World War II to manage power of the sort it had, and the inclination to use military power as a first response has proven unsustainable. This is not the case where a new policy is needed, but rather a new institutional structure to manage a global interest vastly different from World War II. And in the context of this change, other institutional dimensions, domestic as well as international, will have to shift. The problem of foreign policy is a dimension of the general crisis of institutions. The institutional shift will weaken the credibility of the technocracy heading into the 2028 election.

The difficulty in bringing closure to our wars, and the difficulty in adjusting to our new status, flow from the same source. We are governed by people who know a great deal about narrow subjects, but few who can see the whole. The argument can be summed up in Aesop's fable of the fox and the hedgehog. The fox knows many things, while the hedgehog knows one important thing. In order to know many things, the fox must be able to learn quickly. Without that virtue, he would never be able to know all the things he knows. He can therefore learn what he needs to know well enough to get by. But if the fox has to manage a very complex matter, he will fail. The hedgehog can manage any problem in his area of expertise, but the hedgehog can't learn quickly. It takes time to master one big thing.

Another way to look at this is as the difference between knowledge and wisdom. Knowledge is essential, but by itself it is insufficient. The hedgehog knows the one thing he knows, another hedgehog knows the one thing he knows, but who can tie them together? Or who can say which sort of knowledge is more important to have and who has the ability to step back and consider the meaning of all the hedgehogs' knowledge and their impact? The federal government has become the domain of hedgehogs, urgently needed people but profoundly insufficient. It is wisdom that is lacking, and there is no civil service code for the wise.

Many Americans assume that the problem of the federal government is it's too large. The fact is that the growth in the size of the federal government ended in about 1988, a time when it still functioned fairly well.

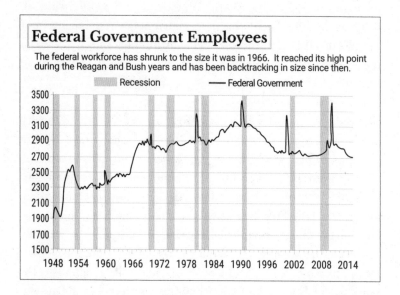

Federal Government Employees

The federal workforce has shrunk to the size it was in 1966. It reached its high point during the Reagan and Bush years and has been backtracking in size since then.

Recession ——— Federal Government

The crisis with the federal government is neither its size nor its mission. The federal workforce has shrunk to the size it was in 1966. It reached its high point during the Reagan and George H. W. Bush years and has been backtracking in size since then. Nor is the problem its mission. Now that the federal government's relationship with the economy and society has shifted, it is no more possible to shift back to the older model than it would be to reverse the relationship between the states and the federal government of the second institutional cycle. The involvement with society will remain in place and will only increase as the threats to American citizens' safety continue.

The problem is the relationship of the federal government to itself. It follows the model created in World War II, of the highly centralized, hierarchical, expert-based system. It is the same model that drove General Motors into bankruptcy. General Motors was superbly managed, if that is judged by the degree of control it had over its internal functions. What it could not do was create a system that was simultaneously creative, not micromanaged, but nevertheless requiring that the parts ultimately constitute a marketable whole. It was not a problem of size, although smaller is easier to manage. There are very large corporations that were able to do this, such as Apple and Goldman Sachs. The legacy companies based on the World War II model either changed or died.

However, the federal government did not evolve. In distributing authority based on specialty, it fragmented itself into countless agencies or informal structures, each obsessed with its narrow function, few able to cooperate effectively with others, and most spending more time struggling with these other entities than performing their function.

By their very incoherence, government actions increase the likelihood that projects will fail, or that they will succeed at an unacceptable cost, or that in succeeding, they will undermine the success of another project. There is no standpoint from which to visualize the whole, and the experts embedded in the nodes of the system are not foxes, nor have they access to the complexity. The result is, from foreign policy to health care, that the convolution of the issue is addressed through solutions that are even more complicated and therefore less understandable.

For example, there were federal agencies designed to facilitate mortgage lending. There were federal agencies responsible for supervising markets. There were federal agencies responsible for monitoring fraud. There were federal agencies responsible for managing the economy. The entire range of the subprime mortgages had federal involvement, but the federal agencies did not work with each other. Had they done so, the problem would have become apparent. But experts in buying mortgages from banks at Fannie Mae, experts in white-collar crime at the FBI, experts at the Securities and Exchange Commission, and experts at the Federal Reserve, all hedgehogs, lacked foxes who know many things. The crash was a surprise to all.

This in turn will continue in the 2020s to create a deeper political problem. It is impossible for the ordinary citizen to understand the complexity of the federal government. This is not because of lack of education or intellect, because it is not fully comprehensible even to those in the government. But to those outside, it is impossible to verify the good intentions or competence of the federal system, and incomprehensibility inevitably leads to distrust. When the term "deep state" is used, it assumes that the federal government is what its proponents assert: a highly rational, integrated, and well-led system. If that is true, then many believe that the things the government undertakes, from failed wars and poorly thought-out surveillance of citizens, to failed poverty programs, must be intentional.

An impenetrable federal government has produced the sort of mistrust the founders wanted to avoid in creating a democratic republic where the public elects representatives and those representatives oversee the functioning of the government. The problem is, as we close the third cycle, the representatives of the public are unable to supervise the operation of the federal government in detail. Four hundred and thirty-five representatives can't possibly understand what is happening, and neither can the office of the president. Each has layers of staffers, but in general the staffers are not trained in the arcane issues involved in foreign and domestic politics. It is actually not a question of size, because the government must naturally be large to oversee a highly complex nation. The problem is over-complexity and convolution, with subgroups of experts who do not cooperate, trust each other, or work well together.

Additional layers of functionaries are created who are increasingly narrow in their perspective and thereby unable to comprehend the experts managing the nodes. But the problem is cultural. Experts can understand and feel solidarity with other experts because each speaks a common language and likely has a shared or similar past. The overseer frequently merges with what he is supposed to oversee, and the elected official, who obviously does not understand the language of the expert, is incapable of executing the responsibilities of his office.

Creating an even worse crisis in the 2020s will be the fact that it will not be possible for the federal government to retreat from its deep involvement with society. It will be impossible because abandoning the relationships would leave too many links broken and too many operations unmanned. How does the government back off protecting its citizens when the threats are seen to be increasing? What would replace Homeland Security and all the initiatives it contains to find threats, without increasing airport screening by programs such as CLEAR that identify travelers by fingerprints or eye measurements? To make things more efficient, new programs of centralized identification and verification must be developed. Just as the shift after the Civil War was irreversible, so too the shift after World War II and after September 11 is irreversible. The complexity of what has been created, along with the realistic need for someone to do what the federal government does, will make anything more than a tactical shift impossible. The problem this poses will underlie all the 2020s. It can be seen in areas such as the rising tension between protecting the safety of American citizens and the invasion of citizens' rights to privacy. These tensions will spill over into becoming social issues, and finally they will become hot political issues—especially around elections—in the coming decade.

Before the third cycle, pre–World War II, the government was run by people whose legitimacy arose from an election and whose appointees were selected based on political skills and loyalty. Their actions were based on political considerations and sometimes operated outside the law. They had close contact with superiors whose job was to get reelected and who therefore found it advantageous to maintain a generally stable system. They were looking for a political outcome, and politics permeated the government. Their advantage was that they were not expected to perfect the nation or the state. Their mission was modest in governing an immodest country.

The key to the first two institutional cycles was using common sense. It was assumed, as in the founding, that there was a layer of American society that through experience and upbringing had developed sufficient common sense to understand the functioning of government. It might not have been the poorest citizens, who lacked the relevant experience and time. It was not necessarily the wealthiest, whose interests might diverge from the collective interest. But there was a layer whose common sense, not expertise in a limited subject, might rule. And these were the elected presidents, congressmen, and judges selected by the people, sufficiently educated to understand the problem and manage the government. The rise of a class based on expertise was a direct attack on common sense as amateurish and insufficient.

This new model after World War II based on the experts managing fragments of a project, while relying on higher levels to understand and integrate what they were doing, created a massive economic and social evolution. But this system at the same time created a profound institutional problem. First, the common sense that oversaw the first phase was marginalized in management. Second, the sum of expertise was less, not greater, than the parts. The experts did not collaborate on the whole, and entire projects became fragmented, with each part working alone. The criticism of the Affordable Care Act was that the experts had constructed a vast document of difficult-to-understand rules and that the rules did not necessarily support each other. Each part might have been technically fine, but common sense would not allow someone to understand it, nor did any one expert understand the whole.

Consider the following example. For most of American history,

Supreme Court justices were generally lawyers but not necessarily previously judges. They were selected for political reasons and because they had common sense. An example in the third cycle was Earl Warren, who was a lawyer who had served in the army in World War I, then was elected a county district attorney. He entered politics, became governor of California, then vice presidential running mate for Thomas Dewey, who lost to Harry Truman. During his third term as governor, he was nominated by Eisenhower to be chief justice of the Supreme Court. He was far from an expert in law, but he had enormous common sense. When *Brown v. Board of Education* came before the Court, he recognized that history required the end of segregation in schools. He also understood that if the Court was to rule properly, it had to be a unanimous vote. Because he had been a politician, he understood that this was not a legal issue but a political issue, and he focused on persuading all members of the Court, including Tom Clark, a southerner, to vote for it. Warren used common sense and political skill, not expertise in the law.

Now compare this with the Supreme Court today. None of the judges have ever held political office. None had ever run a business or farm. All attended either Harvard or Yale Law School (one started at Harvard but transferred to Columbia). All are experts in the law, or, more precisely, all are experts in the current technical controversies over law. They are technicians of law educated at schools that are superb at educating technicians. As a result, there is a deep rigidity and predictability in the Court. None has the skill to force a compromise when compromise is needed. Their definition of the law does not entail the kind of common sense the Warren Court exercised in 1954, but is primarily technical. The rigidity of the Supreme Court therefore is that it is a legal and political institution, now run by technicians, utilizing seemingly nonideological methods for ideological ends. This is a problem that permeates the federal government and makes it increasingly unable to govern. Common sense, the ability to see consequences far removed from the technical issues, has been banished. The Supreme Court does not understand that sometimes abandoning the technical in favor of political common sense is its responsibility.

Certainly, experts are indispensable. They cannot govern, however, because their perspective is limited by their expertise. But as a class they have come to rule the federal government's relation to the United States. Congress passes laws that are basically intentions funded with federal dollars. Experts interpret the intention and create regulations that are intended to implement the intentions. They then administer the regulations. The connection between the intention and the regulation is frequently incidental, but the regulations are so complex and the administration even more so that Congress or the president has no clear idea what is being done. We saw this in the health-care legislation passed during the Obama administration. President Obama meant it when he said his health plan would allow Americans to keep their doctors. The problem is, once the details of the legislation were written (by hundreds of unelected health-care experts), the law became exceptionally difficult to understand and not all participants were, in fact, able to keep their doctors. The intent of the plan by the president and Congress was fairly clear. By the time it was turned into regulations and the regulations applied, many of the outcomes were unintended.

A significant faction of Americans have lost confidence in the federal government through the belief that the technocrats are acting not in the best interests of the citizenry but rather to protect their position and power in government. In a poll taken by the Pew Research Center in April 2019, only about 17 percent of the public claimed to have any degree of confidence in the government. During the Eisenhower years, that number was about 75 percent. It fell to 35 percent during the Carter administration, which was the last presidency of the socioeconomic Roosevelt cycle.

From the public point of view, the federal system is hermetically sealed. Identifying the laws and regulations that might affect you, identifying what the effects might be, managing the system, and controlling your relationship to the federal government are no longer options. Even having a significant impact on the electoral process is difficult.

One of the political crises we will see coming to a peak in the 2020s will be a revolt against the primary system, which empowers minority ideologies and demands large amounts of effort to permit participation. At least 75 percent of the voters are not interested in the primary process, which is what you would expect given the governing ideology that favors private life. Those who tend to vote in primaries are those who are passionate about the elections. Sometimes it is because they take civic responsibility seriously. More often it is that they are passionate about their political beliefs. Because the majority of Americans are not passionate about ideologies, it means that candidates from both parties are selected by a minority who is passionate. Because those who accept the predominant ideology are the ones voting, the candidates are increasingly being selected from the fringe. Particularly in congressional elections, the dedicated ideologues rule.

The primary system has virtually eliminated the presence of the professional party manager on the local level. Prior to World War II, the party boss dominated, determining candidates at all levels. He served two functions: he was ombudsman for citizens in their dealings with government, and he steadied the electoral system. As a professional, his goal was not ideological and political. His power came from winning elections, and that necessarily drew him to a position away from the fringe. As a professional, the party boss saw himself as providing a service to the voters in exchange for their votes.

Bosses were charged with being corrupt, rigging elections, favoring those who supported them, and working outside the process. They worked the system at all levels, helping businesses get government contracts and taking kickback money as their price. In the Bronx, where I grew up, I recall a boss named Charlie Buckley who provided assistance to Irish, Jews, Italians, Puerto Ricans, and African Americans, aware that they might not be equal in the eyes of society but that their votes were. Bosses might have been corrupt, but the primary system has not abolished corruption.

Bosses had the power to cut through inefficiency. Their critics, trying to reform the system, supported an impersonal approach to government-constituent relations in which political loyalty had nothing to do with access. It made access to services more equitable, but with all the controls it needed, it was also more inefficient, and no one could speed up the process or align it with unanticipated needs.

The loss of the party boss meant that no one directly represented the commonsense demands of the public to the government. As he was eliminated, access to the federal system came through formal paths, which citizens could not easily navigate. The congressman's office became the ombudsman for those with enough sophistication to use it, but for most people access was declined. The informal access to government services came at the price of political loyalty, and it strengthened the boss's hold over his party, and the party's hold over the electorate. But it was not clearly undemocratic. The boss was the center of the system, and the affection or at least respect for him was real in most cases because he survived on that, earned by his services.

The movement toward primaries and for the public directly controlling government was a movement against the party bosses and toward honesty in government. But it could not be flexible for those with idiosyncratic needs. The bosses could solve problems in delivering services to the favored—a substantial and open group. Now all were equal, and the delivery of services was designed for that purpose, preventing needed exceptions.

The primary system also polarized politics. It turned candidate selection from a boss-led process to an increasingly ideological one. In the end, this was part of the reason for the downfall of the bosses; ideologues had been excluded. With so few voting in primaries, those who cared the most won. The primary process was thus turned over to the minority of ideologues who would show up on a busy Tuesday, in spite of work or of rain, taking the kids to piano lessons, and cooking dinner. Those who could manage such mundane concerns, or didn't have those concerns, controlled the ballot as rigorously as did the boss.

The new relationship between the citizen and the government that comes into play in the 2020s will not replicate the old political system. Too much has changed for that. But the principle that the political system should both provide solutions to individual, personal problems and generate competent leadership will force a shift. Consider that the old system produced presidents like Abraham Lincoln, Theodore Roosevelt, Woodrow Wilson, Franklin Roosevelt, and Dwight Eisenhower, along with much lesser lights. The point is that measured by outcome, the boss system was certainly no worse than what the primary system produced and perhaps in many ways it was better. But aside from personalities, the boss system focused on serving and mobilizing the nonideological mass, preventing the minority ideologues from controlling the system, and preventing the levels of polarization that have materialized in the past few elections during the later years of the third institutional cycle.

Even more important, consider this from the standpoint of the federal government as an institution. The creation of a rigorously impersonal system, managed by technocrats who prefer to be constrained by process, inevitably leaves many unanticipated needs unsatisfied. There are always special cases that in principle ought to be handled but do not fit into the regulations. Under the bosses, these would be handled by asking him for help and by his making a phone call. That is no longer an option. Nor is there anyone to manage the complexity of the system. The system is honest but inflexible and difficult to navigate. The federal government is a vast machine with limited access, and that access crowded and hard to read.

Neither form of representation has been perfect, and over the next decade—in addition to the other crises coming to a head—this conflict will build into one between expertise and common sense. Expertise will make the valid claim that the issues are complex and need to be managed by experts. Common sense will argue that the methods and solutions used by expertise are incapable of dealing with these issues because the ideal solution, from a practical point of view, takes so long to implement and neglects the citizens' experience so profoundly that expertise only creates the illusion of a solution. Experts will see their critics as ignorant of the facts and incapable of understanding complexity. Their critics will argue that experts are more interested in protecting their positions and authority than in considering the effect they are having. And all of this will be compounded by mutual distrust and disgust.

Over the 2020s, this growing conflict will not be confined to government. The technocracy is as much a social class as a governing body. For example, journalists for traditionally trusted newspapers, which used to be called the prestige press, have lost their standing. A Gallup poll in 2017 showed that only 27 percent of respondents trusted newspapers to any degree. A poll by the American Association for the Advancement of Science found only 14 percent of the public held universities in high esteem. According to Gallup, the most highly trusted institutions are the military at about 75 percent and the police at about 58 percent. The institutions most trusted are those that are perceived to not be drawn from the technocracy. In 2015, a Pew survey showed that only 19 percent of Americans trusted the federal government. It should be noted that these numbers come before Trump's election. The crisis didn't start with Trump, but rather resulted in his presidency, and Trump is someone who senses the distrust and thrives on it. The numbers reflected the confrontation between government, media, and universities, on the one hand, and the emerging opposition, on the other.

If this was the only crisis building in the 2020s, it would be cause for enough concern. But we are also facing a social and economic crisis reaching its peak around the same time, and by then it will become fully entangled with the institutional crisis. As we have discussed in previous chapters, the core of the economic cyclical crisis derives from its very success. Under Reagan, changes in the tax code increased capital available for investment, which, combined with the new core technology, the microchip, created a new economic and social reality. The newly re-created entrepreneurship of the Microsofts and Oracles transformed how the economy worked. A new class of high-tech wealth arose but at the same time contributed to the decline of an old industrial system. Investment flowed into industry to make it more efficient, laying off workers. Later, as the rate of return on investment from microchip-based economies surged while industrial profits stagnated, shifting industrial production to foreign countries led to massive unemployment and underemployment of industrial workers.

Obviously, this situation led and will continue to lead in the next decade to significant anger among the displaced industrial class. It is not only an economic issue. It is also a cultural one. The technocracy, broadly understood, destabilized not only the economic foundations of the industrial working class but also the foundations of its cultural values. The cultural beliefs the industrial workers are taught in church, still a revered institution to them, are not forms of phobia. The federal government, part of the technocracy, sided with and even led this assault on their values, treating the declining industrial class as having little to offer economically or socially.

Trump's election was not the important thing, nor actually were the laid-off workers. Much of this has to do with the systemic shift in economies.

Already there before 2020, this sense of embattlement will increase in the 2020s and extend beyond the federal government. It will extend to the technocracy as a whole because the technocracy shares an ideology that goes beyond simply the belief in expertise. Because it invents new ways of doing things and assumes that progress comes from intellectual activity, the technocracy is also seen as a revolt against tradition and traditional values. In this sense, the technocracy is in keeping with the principles of the founders, save that the founders did not see a tension between technical progress and agriculture. It's not surprising, then, that the technocracy—understood in its broadest sense—will challenge more traditional values, adding to the social tensions of this coming decade.

Where the United States emerges at the end of the decade will in large part depend on how these crisis points are handled by both the voters and the leaders of the nation. How much the United States is ripped apart in the 2020s will depend on the steps taken in particular sectors of American life to rectify the situation and lessen the pain for the people on both sides of the divide: those enduring the economic and social decline, and those technocrats who must be disrupted in order to rebuild an efficient government and public life. To understand that future forecast, we must understand the depth of the crisis coming in two critical sectors of American life: technology and education.

10

The 2020s Crisis in Technology and Education

One of the forces shaping American history has always been technology. That follows from the founding principles and from the need to bind the nation together. Americans differ from each other by personal histories and regional realities. They are bound together by the search for a better life, understood as rooted in economics. For the economy to evolve, then, so must the relationship of Americans to nature. That requires evolution in technology and, in turn, evolution in how Americans learn to create not only new technologies but the businesses that grow from them, the way Americans entertain themselves, and all that follows. This in turn rests on education.

In its broadest sense, technology is the means of changing humanity's relationship with its past and with nature. We've discussed earlier the impact of technologies like electricity that transformed the traditional experience of night, extending the time people had to read and learn and contracting the time they had to sleep and dream. Other technologies took music from the concert hall to the home, available on demand, and took plays and movies from the theater to television, where people could watch from the privacy of their living rooms. Technologies transformed nature and the centuries-old traditions that accompanied it. They also transformed how humans made a living and how well-off they might be. Technology can also frame or even be the battleground of the social and economic struggle. Ever since the Industrial Revolution, the technologist has become a center of wealth, cultural influence, and power.

Technology is certainly at the heart of the Reagan cycle, which began in 1980 and is slowly concluding, both in creating prosperity and in generating the institutional and socioeconomic crises. Each generation has a core technology that throws off endless applications and businesses. The steam engine and electricity both developed multiple applications that permitted other technologies and that changed the economic and personal landscape.

We've talked about America as an invented country. The technologies invented by Americans have also revolutionized the world. Microchips were introduced in the early 1970s for use by the U.S. military and for consumers in the form of pocket calculators. In the early 1980s, numerous first-generation computers were introduced by Texas Instruments, RadioShack, Atari, and many others. By the late 1980s, they had started to become commonplace in the office and, coupled with related products from the printer to the Internet, revolutionized the economy and everyday life. From the mid-1980s until about 2010, the microchip was in its second stage. It then became a mature industry producing new applications and some new innovations, but the second period was over, and with it the dramatic increases in productivity. The microchip was a transformative and core technology. It also reintroduced the tradition of inventors like Edison who combined innovation with business. The big question for the future is, what is the next transformative technology and how do we recognize it in its early form?

Transformative and core technologies go through four stages. The first innovative stage is when the core technology exists but the technologist is trying to perfect it and develop a business around it. The second stage is a working product that evolves in unexpected directions and dramatically increases productivity. The third stage is a mature, enormously useful product that still changes and produces new business models but not at the rate it had in the second stage. Productivity growth from the technology begins to fade. In the fourth stage, the technology continues to be important but ceases to be dynamic. Henry Ford introduced the automobile, a derivative of the internal combustion engine, to the mass market in about 1915. By about 1960, it was mature. It had saturated the market along with competitors, and its basic architecture was in place. Improvements were inevitable within the basic framework. It took about forty-five years from introduction to the mass market to maturity. It took the microchip from about 1980 to 2020 to achieve maturity, again forty years.

This is not to say in any way that the microchip is obsolete. It has transformed our lives, changing how we shop, how we communicate and find information, and even how we think. Since 1980, the microchip has dramatically driven growth in productivity. But now those productivity growth numbers are declining to near zero.

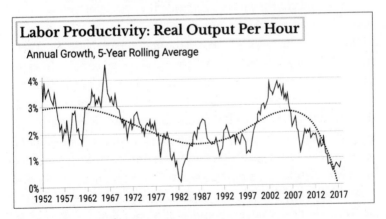

Labor Productivity: Real Output Per Hour

Annual Growth, 5-Year Rolling Average

Note in this graph of labor productivity from the Bureau of Labor Statistics a similarity between the declines of 1962 until 1982 and the decline since the early years of the second decade of the twenty-first century. New technologies are a major factor driving productivity growth, and productivity growth drives the economy. There is nothing new in the maturation of the microchip, including the inability of the culture to imagine maturity and even decline. It is nevertheless painful until a new core technology emerges. And the decade from 2020 to 2030 will already be very painful from the crises caused by the intersection of the two major cycles. Add to it that a core technology is running its course and no new core technology has yet replaced it, and that pain increases.

The heroic phase of the microchip economy generated vast amounts of money, held by financial institutions of various sorts as well as "high net worth" individuals—which is how the rich are referred to these days. Finance has run into a unique problem that will cause additional pain in the 2020s. During the current cycle, a great deal of money was made that flowed to the class that used it for investing rather than consumption. That was the intent, and it worked, producing even more wealth. That money needs to be invested. However, as the decline in start-ups shows, it has become harder to find places to invest. Particularly after 2008, the opportunities for investment have contracted.

We are now in a situation that is the opposite of the 1970s. Then there was a capital shortage. Now there is a capital surplus. Interest rates are historically low not because the central bank's policies make it so. They contribute to it. But the fundamental problem is that there is a tremendous pool of money available for investment and a contracting number of microchip-based business opportunities to invest in. Investment therefore looks in other directions that are more traditional, including health care and retail, but it's not cutting-edge technology. This pool of money looks for safe alternatives in bonds, keeping the price of money down and creating a massive problem for all retirees, but particularly those from the aging industrial sector, already drained of their resources. What little assets they have will no longer bring any significant earnings, thus intensifying the pressure on them.

The industrial working class had the ability to be a powerful force in the 2016 election but not to force the agenda in Congress. They are a declining class and don't have the ability to move the economic and social system back to the time when they prospered. They lack the numbers, and there is no returning to robust industrialism. As this class ages in the 2020s, it faces extremely difficult times, and it also loses what strength it had. This is not the class that will challenge the technocracy.

The ones who will challenge the technocracy in the coming decade will be the children and grandchildren of the industrial class who themselves have had no contact with industrialism beyond family memories, were raised in fairly difficult conditions, and face a grim future without a significant change in their circumstances. The vanguard of this movement will be those born from about 1990 to 2010, who will be between twenty and forty in 2030. In a sense, these will be the millennials who do not live in Manhattan or San Francisco and do not work in marketing or high tech. They are the millennials who don't fit the clichés of the dominant culture.

The emerging transformations of the 2020s crisis will revolve around the institutions of education. How we educate and whom we educate will be bound up with technology. All the threads of the technocracy lead back to the university, from financial engineers, filmmakers, government officials, judges, to technology marketers. Individuals get three things in the university. The first is a broad array of knowledge that will allow them to enter a field, accumulate more knowledge, and succeed. The second are credentials. In the initial critical phase of a career, the questions asked are, what did you major in and where did you go to college? The answer to what you majored in gives a sense of your focus; the answer to where you went to college generates a perception of your quality of mind. Going to a satellite campus of the state university of a small state generates one kind of perception. Not going to college at all gives no credentials. There are those who succeed in spite of that, but they are few. (Bill Gates's credentials were not undermined when he dropped out of Harvard because, after all, he had been admitted to Harvard.) The third thing individuals get at university is the opportunity to develop the connections that may support them throughout their lives. The right school and the right friends can sustain a career. The wrong school can strand you or make the battle uphill all the way. The right school will teach you the manners and values that integrate you into the technocracy. The wrong school won't.

The issue now and during the next decade is access to the center of gravity of the technocracy, the leading universities that not only teach subjects but train you in the social rituals that allow you to belong to the technocracy. Those universities are increasingly closed to those who didn't descend from this group. In pre–World War II America, the best universities were regarded as havens for the elite; back then, it was the moneyed white Anglo-Saxons and Protestants. World War II smashed those barriers with the GI Bill. Universities were radically democratized and created a social revolution that drove the Roosevelt cycle, opening the door to the elite.

The emergence of two different cultures will intensify in the 2020s. Already visible is the culture of technocracy, in which merit is defined by top universities and expectations on marriage and family will continue to deviate from historical norms in various ways. Above all, the technocrats will insulate themselves from the social and political upheaval by enclosing themselves in a sense of moral excellence complementing their technical excellence. The "outsiders" will live in a sense of desperation and anger and will also experience the shift in marriage and family but as a social crisis.

As this crisis builds, at the center of the opposition will be the children of the white industrial working class, particularly those born after the year 2000, for whom the comfortable life of the middle class will be only a memory. They will be joined by unanticipated allies from among those who share needs and backgrounds: African Americans, Hispanics, and others will identify themselves less by their identities than by their needs. Identity politics, which emerged from the legal concept of "protected classes" in federal social design, is unsustainable. As the children of the white working class find themselves in the same position as African Americans, a more traditional social struggle will emerge, based on exclusion of the lower class. It will create alliances that are unthinkable today.

Identity protection left most of this group outside the places where knowledge and credentials came from—including all identities because most African Americans did not benefit from being "protected." The politics of identity cannot solve problems rooted in the inflexibility of institutions, in this case universities. Racial conflict is endemic to the United States. The tensions between American whites and African Americans have been woven into the fabric of American history. The rising racial tensions we've seen in the past few years are bound to increase during the 2020s–2030s because of the pressures from the crises in the other areas we've been examining. Families and individuals facing economic hardships, cultural assaults, and a government and class of leaders that seem indifferent won't be silent.

The only bridge there can be is one of common interest, as there was during the New Deal. Interestingly, that common interest is returning. Hispanics will rise socially and economically on their own due to the dynamics of wave after wave of immigration, of which they are part. They will have only a passing interest in this new coalition. But African Americans need another way to a comfortable life and some wealth other than the path technocracy offers. And the children of the industrial working class are thought of as the moral descendants of the Scots-Irish, a class that was once despised. Because this class is about 30 percent of the American population while African Americans are 13 percent, it is a powerful coalition bound by common interests and not sentiment. It will be a strange and uneasy alliance, of course, but one with precedence.

The crisis in the universities has not happened overnight. For several generations, it had been possible to get into the best school with good grades and SAT scores. The best universities, assailed by an army of high school seniors with excellent grades and SAT scores, sought for ways to distinguish among them. They searched for students who had not merely done well in high school but shown some exceptional talent, or social awareness. The operant phrase was that they were searching for students "who would benefit most" from attending their schools. With so many who might benefit because they did well in high school, the universities looked for more qualifiers.

It began with focusing on the letters written by students explaining why they wanted to attend a certain school. Those who were most verbal and could surprise the admissions committee with a startling idea were of course ahead of the pack. How many of these letters were written by parents or even paid admissions coaches is unknown, but there are startlingly few seventeen-year-olds who could have written the kinds of letters that I read sitting on admissions committees. Those who had access to adults capable of writing, or at least coaching the writing of such letters, had a huge advantage.

The next step in the culling process was extracurricular activities. Doing well in school and on the SATs being insufficient, admissions committees looked for students who spent their spare time doing worthwhile things. Students are judged by whether they have worked for a charity helping poor people in places such as Peru, internships they might have held with their congressman, tutoring poor children, or having won awards perhaps as a musician. Whether being a missionary teaching conservative Christian values to Bolivians would exact enthusiasm from the admissions committee is another and nontrivial matter. But there is a more significant issue.

Many students have no time for extracurricular activities because they are working on a construction site to help out their family or flipping hamburgers for pocket money. When in high school,

I had no time for a nonpaying summer internship at a financial house. I had to earn money during the summer. The children of the industrial class cannot afford to travel as volunteers to a construction site in Haiti on behalf of Habitat for Humanity, even if they had sponsors for the travel costs. They need to earn money to pay their college fees, support themselves, or help their family. Whether Habitat for Humanity would be the charity they chose to support rather than a local charity based at their church is an important topic. But the most important topic is whether they can afford the nonpaying extracurricular activities that top universities expect. Some schools recently began to claim that they regard after-school work as an extracurricular activity. Perhaps so, but will they value work in a congressman's office gained by a parent's contribution to his campaign as they do working at Walmart? And if they do, will they be believed? Credibility in equality is the core issue.

The selection process at the best schools is presently designed not to find the best minds but rather to find minds already shaped to the culture and ideology the universities regard as being able to benefit from their education. As we reach the end of these current institutional and socioeconomic cycles, the universities have reconstructed the walls that existed before the GI Bill and the New Deal. Elite colleges are admitting primarily those students whose social background allows them to provide an application profile that fits what the universities regard as "their kind of student," much as it was in the 1920s. On the margins, they accept students of protected classes who may well deserve to be there on their own merits. What is excluded are the children of the predominantly white industrial class.

For children of the declining industrial class going to a college well below the elite, the chances of meeting those who can help you in upward mobility are slim. Colleges don't simply teach you skills. They socialize students into the culture of the world they will be entering and introduce them to others who are already part of that culture. This is no different from an immigrant going to the Ivies in the 1920s. And that is the point. The declining class is not immigrants. The political consequences of that fact are massive. If you want to be a Google engineer or a partner at Goldman Sachs, Stanford and Harvard are the places to be, and the dynamics of the cycles have made these universities the property of those who meet the social and cultural norms.

Harvard University is quite blunt about this, I'm sure without intending to be. Acknowledging that some might not have had the opportunities for extracurricular activities due to family and financial problems, Harvard asks these students what they would want to do with their free time, requiring them to anticipate the unknown opportunities. The critical criteria Harvard lists are these:

> Would other students want to room with you, share a meal, be in a seminar together, be teammates or collaborate in a closely-knit extracurricular group?

In other words, will you fit in? Will your peers value you? Eighteen- and nineteen-year-olds have never been known for their social flexibility. That is what a university should teach them. And above all, what should be valued are those who are dramatically different. After World War II, Harvard welcomed a generation that could never fit in to its crowd. Now Harvard is once again looking for the right sort of fellow, as in an F. Scott Fitzgerald novel. This will only add fuel to the fires that are already smoldering. In the coming decade, the United States will face a crisis of education and opportunity ignited by the economic and social pressures of the two cycles colliding.

But the educational crisis will not be only over entrance to universities. There is another major financial problem that has become part of the economic cycle's crisis, even though many don't yet realize it. Attending Harvard University—including tuition, room, and board—can cost about $70,000 per year, and closer to $80,000 when factoring in textbooks, health coverage, and other essentials. Harvard is a wealthy school and can afford to help poorer students who qualify for financial aid or scholarships. State schools like Ohio State at the Columbus campus for tuition, room, and board costs a state resident about $23,000 a year, and adding in books and healthcare it's close to $25,000 per year. This is far less than Harvard, but still $100,000 over four years. Law school, medical school, business school, costs even more. It used to be possible to work your way through college. Even at a state school, that would now be extremely difficult. There are, of course, student loans and some grants available, but borrowing to pay for college can leave the student financially crippled for years, making upward mobility an abstraction. A student loan is basically a gamble on graduating and entering the elite of the technocratic class with a well-paying job very quickly. And for many students, the only schools they can get into don't hold open that possibility.

The cost of the universities is stunning and can't be sustained. To give some sense of the cost, the total amount of student debt is now $1.34 trillion. To benchmark this, total mortgage debt today is $8.4 trillion, and in 2008 the total amount borrowed in subprime mortgages was also $1.3 trillion. Just as mortgage derivatives were bundled and sold, that is happening now with student loans. Where mortgages were bought by Fannie Mae and Freddie Mac, both federal entities designed to provide liquidity in the mortgage market, so Sallie Mae, the federal equivalent for student loans, is buying, bundling, and reselling student loans.

Whatever the underlying issues, most cycles end or begin in financial crisis. The student loan crisis won't be the subprime crisis of 2008, but that is a substantial amount of money, with the average student borrowing about $35,000 during his college term, and poorer students at state colleges borrowing the most, because they start with the least. They will also make far less than a Harvard graduate, which means that there is a subprime class developing. But not going to college guarantees a worse outcome, because without those credentials these students are mostly locked out of any upward mobility.

Why a college education is so expensive has two dimensions. First, many college campuses, particularly of elite universities, are well-manicured parks. I did my graduate work at Cornell, an extraordinarily beautiful place I enjoyed very much, ranging from its racquetball court to its lakes. No sane student would be unhappy there, but the cost of building and maintaining a college campus is staggering. Moreover, the value of the university properties, if they were sold, would make a serious dent in the student loan problem. There is no inherent reason why a college education requires such facilities. I attended CCNY in New York, with an austere campus, as well as Cornell. I did not notice that Cornell's delightful campus stimulated my intellect any more than did CCNY.

The second problem is that being a university professor is among the highest-paid part-time work in the world. The average semester lasts about thirteen to fourteen weeks. Assuming a week spent grading, the average tenured professors work six months out of the year. During this period in elite schools, they may teach one or two classes a week, about six hours in the classroom or as much as twelve hours a week in the least prestigious. The professor is teaching a subject he is an expert in, so over time preparation approaches zero hours, and in universities with graduate programs the grading is done by graduate students. The professor is expected to do research and publish, and some do, while others, with tenure, do less. But there is also a question of whether what is published has any real value. I have in my past career published a number of academic articles whose social utility was invisible.

Universities understand the unsustainable cost of this system and reduce that cost by using adjunct professors—people with the ability to teach but unable to get a permanent, full-time job. The adjunct professors scramble for whatever jobs they can get at strikingly low wages and essentially fill the gap between what is needed and what can be afforded. The adjunct professor positions are far less prestigious than tenured professorships, but it is not clear that they know less or teach more poorly than full-time professors, although it is likely true that their skills diminish over time due to the tenuousness of their lives. But the university, when it must control costs, finds a way of doing so without disturbing the tenured faculty.

My point is not to trash the university. It is indispensable. It is also unsustainable in its present form. The cost of higher education can no longer be sustained. The problem of cutting costs while increasing capacity and quality is as important a problem as ending the capital shortage under Reagan or unemployment under Roosevelt. Core to alleviating the social and economic problems in the 2030s is utilizing the population and re-creating upward mobility. The university is at the heart of both the problem and the solution. It also becomes the center of a political battle.

This startling piece of information from *The Atlantic* is worth considering:

> In 2016, out of the 160,000 people enrolled in a group of 36 top-flight undergraduate programs, *just 645*—or about 0.4 percent—of them were veterans.

The elite universities are not, I expect, limiting veterans for ideological reasons. They are limiting them because their conception of what a student should be like is so heavily skewed toward the children of those who are like the managers of the university that they have entirely lost the mission they were given after World War II, not only to educate the veterans, but to create a path to upward mobility for those who are not just like them. And I suspect that most veterans would not consider applying to the top schools because they understand that they would not be accepted and would not belong there.

It should not be surprising that the university has become the basic issue, because it follows from the 1787 Northwest Ordinance that was introduced by Thomas Jefferson in 1784, requiring every new state to fund a university. Jefferson and his colleagues believed that the development of such universities would create a learned class of farmers and merchants, contributing to the development of the economy and establishing the basis of democracy. The graduates of these universities would serve as the educated leaders of their community and as inventors of the future.

The university is the battleground of the crisis of the 2020s because it is the system that fuels the broad social bureaucracy. If the social bureaucracy is going to change, it must first happen with a change in the universities. The new influx of students is there for two reasons. The first is to gain the knowledge and credentials they need to enter the technocracy. The second is to change the technocracy because its cultural assumptions are divergent to those of its opponents. And if the cultural pattern of the technocracy shifts, its values shift, and so does how it operates. And that will lead to a transformation of institutions, public and private, just as an evolution in technology will restart the growth of productivity and therefore the economy. The issue of how the university looks is really about how the technocracy will look.

And this transformation will have as its other driver a crisis in student loans that dramatically changes the economics of university life. With student loans, universities have been able to raise the price of education while maintaining their methods and limiting the number of students they need to have in order to sustain them. If student loans cease to be readily available in the future, the only solution will be cutting expenses or increasing the number of students admitted at lower cost. The schools whose credentials are most valuable may not be in this bind, but the rest will be, and in time even the elite universities will be caught up in it. Out-of-the-box thinking and acting will be needed during the crisis of the 2020s. Many universities are on extraordinarily valuable land that could be sold, the teaching load could be increased so long as a more demanding definition of what constitutes research is provided, and the reduction of student loan availability along with more rigorous credit standards will force the university to open its doors.

The coalition that put Roosevelt into power consisted of northern ethnic groups, rural southerners, and African Americans. The coalition that put Reagan into power was small- and large-business people coupled with a significant part of union labor. As cycles transition, the insurgent coalition is a very odd mixture. Southern racists and African Americans will make a strange coalition, as did the alliance of corporate Americans with union workers. The coalition will be built not on love but on necessity. The pressures generated by the last cycle's failure will force a coalition that seems unlikely. It was less cooperation than separately reacting to different aspects of the same failure. But what it did do in both cases with Roosevelt and Reagan was to force a major realignment of political factions and create massive tension over that realignment. Roosevelt's victory changed the dynamics of American politics, as did Reagan's, and the response, particularly from those losing power, was vitriolic.

We have seen the same vitriol emerge in the 2016 election, both from those supporting and from those opposing Trump. Voters in the Midwest who had been historically Democratic shifted in sufficient numbers to tilt the Electoral College and the election. The vitriol on all sides grew to extreme proportions. Trump was the target of the critics and the hero of his supporters.

In previous cycles, the vitriol rose and fell during the period between the beginning of the shift and the decisive presidency. For example, after the resignation of Richard Nixon, there was a period of uneasy calm. It was when Reagan was elected that the contempt began again, focusing on Reagan's policies as a betrayal of the values of the last political cycle. But it also focused on Reagan, charging that he was intellectually incapable of functioning as president and simply a creation of the media and marketing. So too we can expect the vitriol to die down when Trump leaves office and an uneasy calm to exist. Then, following the election of 2028, a new explosion, as the incoming president's radical policies—from the standpoint of the prior half a century—come under attack. But this vitriol will be simply the surface of the deep structural changes.

For the next dozen years or so, the technocrats will continue to rule, increasingly self-enclosed, increasingly contemptuous of challenges, and increasingly weakening. Given demography, they will continue to control the federal government, less through the electoral process than through their control of the system of government. They will continue to focus on the issues that could be seen in the Clinton campaign, which was the quintessential technocratic argument: education, experience, and credentials providing a governing system focused on the deserving poor and also on the social values of technocracy.

Throughout this period of the 2020s, the economic pain will increase, felt most by the industrial workers, who will sink from middle class to lower-middle class. They will lose even the minimal elements of American success in homes, vacations, tuition for children in college. These will slip away from them and from their children. The technological gap between the microchip and the follow-on core technology will continue to cut into productivity and continue to discourage investment. It will be a period in which the technocracy will continue to live well, while the rest of the country stagnates at best and more likely declines.

When the election of 2028 comes, the technocrats will be shocked at the outcome, and when the new government takes control, they will be stunned at the speed at which the assumptions they have lived by are overthrown. Because this happens once every fifty years, there will be a layer of the population who saw and remembers the events of 1980, which resulted in overthrowing domestic and foreign policy and turned the contempt that greeted Reagan into shock at what followed. And what follows will, as with Roosevelt and Reagan, maintain the core principles of America while radically changing how we experience it.

During the 1920s, there were alternatives to a university degree. There were jobs to be had and small businesses to start. That was no longer true during the 1930s. The alternative was to either open the institutions of the elite to the poor or create a permanent underclass. World War II and the GI Bill solved the dilemma. That dilemma is back. Either the rapidly declining white working class will gain access to the credentials needed to rise, or a permanent underclass will be created. The danger in the 1930s of such a class was real, as it is now.

Interestingly, those who are successful hold both classes in contempt. But one of the powerful aspects of American society is that those who are economically desperate and socially displaced get to vote, and those who will be falling into the abyss are not a small marginal class but a large, multiracial, multiethnic class containing equal numbers of women and men. Their actions are inevitable and the results obvious. The universities, the center of gravity of the technocracy, will become the battleground of this crisis whose fate will ultimately be determined by the federal government. This will be doubly the case when the $1.3 trillion student debt problem begins driving the financial markets.

For most of the 2020s, the driving economic force will be low growth in productivity, decreased opportunities for investment of accumulated capital, and low interest rates. It will also be a period of increasing unemployment, driven by continued decline in industry and stagnation in high tech as the result of the maturation of the core technology. Psychologically, the stagnation in the demand for tech workers will be more stunning than the continuation of the

decline in industry, because reversals caused by technology's maturation are always destabilizing socially. In the 1960s, the decline of
the American auto industry was unthinkable, and stunning when it
occurred in the 1970s. There will of course be the normal business
cycle working in the framework of these realities, but the booms will
be less noisy and the troughs deeper. This is the norm at the end of
a cycle.

The social structure will be destabilized as well. I've already
discussed the sequence of generations in the industrial class, but
the technocracy will be under heavy pressure as well. The federal
government will find it increasingly hard to function, and the norm
is to blame the federal employee for a systemic problem. The universities will be under attack for their class biases, inefficiencies, and the
attempt to cope with the de-leveraging of the student loan bubble.
Those in the high-tech sector will find themselves far less glamorous
or easily employed than before. The financial sector, the most agile
of the group, will be restructuring to profit from the new reality.

The industrial class, now the children of the generation that lost
their standing, will be making demands but will not have the political weight to do it themselves. There must be a coalition to have
the weight to force change. That coalition will be an unlikely one,
but it will include all those who experience the current structure
as hostile to their interests. It will, for example, come to include
African Americans, most of whom continue to be excluded, unless
they are able to present themselves as almost like those in the university. The brilliant African American graduating from an ordinary
high school and with few noteworthy extracurricular activities will
have the same chance of getting into an elite university as his white
counterpart.

The political system reflects and magnifies the shifting social
patterns at first, then settles down into an apparently stable pattern
before facing a terminal crisis and the end of the cycle. The cadence
will be announced in presidential elections in 2024 and 2028, which

both frame the cyclical shift and are the reflection of the underlying reality. The institutional and economic and social shifts will merge together in these elections.

The Trump election announced the coming end of this cycle, in an election that signaled both a radical shift and utter gridlock in the system. It was driven by the industrial working class aligned with ideological and economic allies, but the technocracy remained intact and therefore had the strength to balance the Trump administration politically.

The technocrats are obsessed with returning the system to the norm that they are used to and think of as the natural condition. The 2020 election, if it follows patterns, ought to be won by the technocracy, which means the Democrats, although in fact it is an election that can go either way and not significantly affect the process.

The 2024 election will be the critical one because it will elect the last president of the Reagan cycle. As with Jimmy Carter or Herbert Hoover, the president will face significant economic and social problems, and what he will do is apply the basic principles of the Reagan era: lowering taxes and reducing regulations. This will be the case with either party. But the problem that the Reagan presidency was solving was capital shortage, and lower taxes helped with this. The problem at the end of the Reagan cycle is that capital has successfully expanded, but is no longer able to drive the economy, and has left a large part of society increasingly unequal. The solutions imposed will make matters worse rather than solve the problem.

And that will lead to the election of 2028 that will introduce radical new principles to American governance, both institutional and socioeconomic. The election will be politically decisive, bringing in a president by a significant majority as well as a supporting Congress. The last presidency of the Reagan era will act as a slingshot to the new period. Ronald Reagan knew what he would do when he became president, which was cut taxes. Franklin Roosevelt did not know what he would do, but he improvised. The result will be not what the president thinks he is going to do but what he will be compelled by reality to do and by those who will elect him. We have seen the problem and the coalitions that will form. Now we must consider what the solution looks like as we move out of the storm and into the calm.

11

Beyond the Storm

New cycles are often disorderly at the beginning until they sort out and transition to the new solutions. Consider the 1930s or 1970s, each of which was on one side or another of a socioeconomic shift. Each was followed by an era that began an extended period of prosperity. Institutional shifts are normally preceded by military conflict, with that conflict's end creating the foundation for a new institutional structure. But out of this crucible will emerge both a new socioeconomic and a new institutional system. The 2020s will be a period of failures. The 2030s and beyond will be a period of creation.

The election of 2028 (2032 at the outside) will create the political framework for moving beyond the storm of the prior decade. As we enter the sixth socioeconomic cycle, the political battle will be between the now frayed and reactionary technocrats, who will continue to assert that their expertise, credentials, and merit make them the morally legitimate power in the United States. Their challengers will be a coalition that comprises the heirs of the dispossessed of the prior cycle, who will move beyond the ethnic divisions that dominated the previous cycle. This coalition will demand, as is normally the case, a shift in the distribution of power and wealth, but in doing so will be redefining once again the social landscape of

America. The new socioeconomic cycle will be joined by the next institutional shift.

The challenge in the fourth institutional cycle is how to transform a federal government that is entangled with all aspects of society and no longer functions effectively. The problem must be solved, and the solution will be to introduce a new governing principle to the system. Oddly, it will be a principle that is already part of a vast federal system, the largest bureaucracy of all: the military. In the military, there is the principle of commander's intent. The commander lays down his intention to a certain level and then expects subordinates to apply that with awareness of the reality he is facing. Subordinates are not free to deviate from the intent. Nor are they free to apply the intent mechanically regardless of the reality they encounter. The commander is responsible for making his intent not only clear but understood. He then seeks to reach his intended goal by devolving initiative to his junior officers and NCOs. This is not true of all armies. For example, the Soviet army was a technocratic army. But the U.S. Army was always an army that demanded initiative based on intent.

The idea of a federal government that operates on intent and not on rigidly engineered rules seems counter to all American principles of governance, by not treating everyone and every case the same and by placing power in the hands of junior administrators. An example is that when they landed at Normandy in 1944, American forces encountered hedgerows that trapped them, making it impossible to advance. The intent was to move rapidly into France and surround the Germans. Sergeant Curtis G. Culin, discussing the problem with members of his unit, imagined a solution, which was to put blades on a tank and cut through the hedgerow. Without asking for permission, he modified a tank and discovered it worked. He violated several rules including modifying a very expensive tank without permission. General Omar Bradley saw the innovation, couldn't imagine reprimanding him, gave him the Legion of Merit, and ordered tanks refitted with Culin's solution. Bradley's intent was known to his forces. Culin, understanding the intent, acted on it in an unexpected way that was the key to breaking out of Normandy.

Freedom of action based on commander's intent means that the expectation is success, not a particular way of achieving success. TSA is tasked with preventing terrorists from destroying airlines and killing passengers. The technocratic solution is to apply the same process of examination to all passengers. But governing by intent would allow a TSA employee to allow a ninety-year-old woman in a wheelchair to pass through security without excessive discomfort, based on the TSA official's application of the principle of intent. The intent is to prevent tragedies, and in the judgment of the TSA employee who has far more experience in the matter than the TSA manual, the old lady is unable to cause such a tragedy. Intent is achieved; the engineering solution is dispensed with. The argument will be that allowing initiative might allow a terrorist to slip through. Another idea is the deadening routine of an engineering solution could allow that as well.

Consider another example. When I turned sixty-five, I knew I was eligible for Medicare. I was working and covered by private insurance and saw no reason to switch and make the government pay for my medical expenses. I discovered two years later that I was not merely eligible for Medicare; I was required to take it. When I went to sign up, I was told that I would have to pay a penalty for the rest of my life. For me the penalty was annoying but not significant. But what happens if my circumstances change and it becomes a burden? I was told that someone could file a request for exemption, which, based on income and other factors, might or might not be granted under the rules. So, someone who made the same mistake that I made, and was less fortunate than I was, would have to start paying the penalty, fill out the form, and wait for a reply. The intent of the Social Security Administration was to penalize those who failed to sign up at sixty-five, but only those for whom the penalty would not be a hardship. Understanding the intent, the person handling my situation could quickly say no dice to me yet let others off the hook without going through a complex process (those forms are amazing) and waiting period to achieve the same end while creating a huge hardship for them.

The problem of the third institutional cycle is that the hyper engineering of the technocrats created very rational solutions in general, but only at the cost of ignoring the endless idiosyncrasies that life consists of. Large corporations can hire lobbyists to change the engineering process itself. But individuals have no recourse. They have lost the political boss who interfaced with the government. The price for honesty is impotence. The technocrats' alternative creates the reality of unanticipated harm and inflexibility in managing a society that from its founding is all about flexibility without excluding the possibility of corruption. There is no recourse to the regulations that have been engineered, and the operators of the system are not free to exercise initiative based on commander's intent.

In the fourth institutional cycle as I see it the technocratic approach will be dramatically modified to permit the intent of government to be rationally administered by each level. Rather than vast regulations that few have read and fewer have understood, the concept of common sense will have to be reintroduced. The rigidity of the engineering approach to government fails to anticipate the all-important exceptions and fails to empower the citizen to petition his government in a human way and to a human being. During Lincoln's administration, petitioners, ordinary citizens, waited outside his office hoping for favors of redress. That has by now become impossible until redress of grievances guaranteed to citizens is confined to "rage against the system." The military model offers one solution to this problem.

The other main challenge we will face at the beginning of the fourth institutional cycle is finding a solution to the university as the central battleground as explained in the last chapter. Transforming universities will be as important as finding a new governing principle for the federal government. Most universities are subsidized in some way by the federal government, the most lavish being federally guaranteed student loans. The existence of these loans permits the universities to increase tuition and other costs knowing that student loans will scale with them. This raises the amount that students have to repay and the size of the liability of the federal government. Being eligible for government grants or even free tuition at a small number of elite universities doesn't change the fact that student loans are the standard payment method for those whose parents can't afford tuition.

The first battle will be over student loans, which now constitute an amount larger than the subprime pool of 2008. The end or modification of the student loan system will suddenly limit not only how much universities can raise costs but whether they can maintain them. Universities will have to cut extravagant costs. Vast amounts of money can be raised by selling extraordinarily valuable land and moving into simpler quarters. A visit to a European university will reveal Spartan quarters when compared with most American universities.

More money can be saved by drawing a line between teaching faculty and research faculty. Taken as a whole, most American professors do no or little significant research. Contrary to myth, you can be a very effective teacher without having published a significant article. The teaching load for these teachers must expand further, thus cutting costs. Research programs are normally funded not through university operating funds but by government or foundation money, and much of this money is siphoned off for operating expenses. Money intended for research will go for research. Teaching professors can focus on teaching excellence and not feel as though they have to do pseudo research for appearances.

The loss of fantastically expensive facilities and the creation of a division of labor among faculty appear to be extremely radical changes. Generating entrepreneurial challenges to major corporations also seemed radical during the fifth socioeconomic cycle. The GI Bill seemed radical in the fourth cycle, and the creation of a pure gold standard was radical in the third. Shaping banking laws around the needs of western settlers was radical in the second. And the entire idea of the United States was radical in the first cycle. All cycles change something that seems unshakably permanent. In an age of knowledge, the entity that produces and teaches knowledge has to be changed. It's business as usual for the United States.

The university struggle will be an ideological struggle that will define the politics of the sixth socioeconomic cycle. By politics I don't mean left and right, although the ideas of modern liberalism have intersected the ideology of technocracy. The university is the home of technocracy in the sense that it nurtures expertise and credentials as a basis for judging merit and is constructed in such a way that there is a hierarchy of credentials. The number of students admitted is also limited by space and the restrictions on professorial time. A Spartan space makes the number of seats greater and increases expectations on teaching professors' capacity. Indeed, it will make possible the hiring of more professors, thus further increasing capacity. Harvard admits about two thousand students a year. Why not five thousand? Of course, if it admitted that many, the prestige of Harvard would decline, but not necessarily the knowledge imparted to students.

The university's ideology ultimately rests on its pride of place, the status it occupies, and need rarely justify itself. What are called elite universities frequently can't define the way in which the knowledge they provide is in any way superior to "lesser" schools. They point to research done, which matters but is not inherently superior. Upward mobility can be achieved in two ways: opening elite universities, as happened with the GI Bill, or challenging the claim of being elite, and thereby, in revaluing them rationally, creating a more realistic map of excellence and making a degree from a university like Stanford or Harvard not materially different from a degree from Texas State in terms of quality. Over time that will break the tendency of the socially connected to have their social status affirmed at Stanford or Harvard. Two benefits accrue. First, upward mobility is facilitated by stripping the dubious claim that a Yale or Harvard education is superior to other schools and shifting the credential values. Second, it would permit different classes to mix more freely, as they did in and after World War II. And that would explode the barriers.

Focusing on the university as the battleground of this cycle's crisis may seem odd. Yet the university is increasingly controversial simply in its internal values and emphasis on ethnic, but not necessarily intellectual, diversity. But that is not the shift that will take place. What will happen is an assault on the system that limits upward mobility. And this battle will ultimately change the shape of American society.

The university issues are intimately related to the development of technology, something we will turn to in thinking about what the world will look like economically and socially between 2040 and 2080 and how the institutional framework will look for the rest of the century. We will move from the emergence of the new cycle to its maturity.

Paralleling the emergence of the fourth institutional cycle in the 2030s will be the emergence of the sixth socioeconomic cycle. Let's remember the problems this new cycle will be dealing with that are being created during the end of the fifth socioeconomic cycle. It's important to look at them not as accidents or misjudgments but rather as the consequences of success. When you are building a pyramid, you must plan each layer by choosing the right time to begin structuring the next layer.

Each socioeconomic cycle is, when it reaches maturity, a golden age, with a diamond at its center. Golden ages and diamonds are a dangerous metaphor, but when we think of the evolution of the United States, each cycle had within it a unique characteristic that transformed the United States and a pivotal moment toward which the cycle was building.

Consider the fifth cycle and the 1990s, the sparkling moment in which the microchip showed its hand, the Soviet Union collapsed, and American power towered over the world. Politics and social tensions simmered but didn't explode.

Consider the 1950s in the fourth cycle, where jets, televisions, and interstate highways transformed the geography of the country, letting Americans see things that had been invisible to them and letting them go to places that had been impossibly far away. A decade of Eisenhower's superb banality.

We can see back to the 1890s of the third cycle, when the United States became the largest industrial power in the world; the 1840s of the second cycle, when the geography of the United States was completed; or the first decade of the nineteenth century, of the first cycle, when Louisiana became part of America and the roads to the West were cut through the Appalachians.

After the transition into the new cycle, a golden age emerged, with a small but startling diamond that glittered at its heart. The rest of the era was defined by these moments. The questions facing us are, what will be golden about the sixth cycle, and what will be the diamond at its center?

A golden age doesn't mean a time of universal harmony or a time of unlimited joy or an absence of tragedy. We are humans, and tragedy, suffering, and rage are inescapable. A golden age is an age that in spite of all the pains that are normal and possible nevertheless creates something extraordinary. We think of Athens or the Renaissance as a golden age. Each was suffused with the human condition, from slavery to poverty to war, intrigue, and murder. But these things are common to all times. What we remember about the golden ages in history is not what was common to all times but what was unique to them. What was unique to the United States has been the constant resurrection of the extraordinary, the cyclical reemergence of something that places another, golden layer on the pyramid, in spite of the eternal unhappiness, anger, and poverty that lurked beneath that layer. And what is extraordinary is the extent to which, during these times, these negative and painful things are mitigated if not eliminated. At the end and beginning of each cycle, there is the sense of failure and disaster. Yet each time the United States has re-created itself, perhaps imperfectly, but with a rebirth of startling superiority.

The diamond moment that defines the golden age seems to come two or three decades after the new cycle begins. That means that we are looking forward to the 2050s or 2060s. Until then, we will be building the structure of the sixth socioeconomic cycle, and after that golden age the inevitable decline will begin. In order to grasp the future cycle, we need to understand when that moment will be, and to do that, we must understand the way the problems we have seen will define themselves.

The financial problem that will frame the sixth cycle is a surplus of money in the economic system and its distribution. The surplus arose from the success of the fifth cycle and the maturation of the microchip economy. As I've mentioned several times, the big issue is lots of available money and not enough opportunities to invest in things that create wealth. The money is unevenly distributed, clustered in the upper half of society and increasing its concentration the higher you go. Given low interest rates on money, it makes little sense to hold that money in banks or in bonds that pay low interest. Rather than holding money, investors decide to buy things, such as real estate. Therefore, home prices, commercial real estate, and rental properties are surging in price. This is creating the problem for those living beneath median income. They have not shared in the wealth that has been created, at least not evenly, and as prices

GEORGE FRIEDMAN

on real estate rise, they are unable to buy, and in the lower-middle classes they are often unable even to rent.

The dominant political forces will be those beneath median income and those in the upper quarter, with the rest being between the two. There will also be an ideological realignment of a retreating Reagan-era free-market group, a resurgent class who are focused on outcome, and the outcome they will want is a redistribution of income and even of already earned wealth. The culture wars that define politics in the fifth cycle will continue but will no longer be linked to economic demands and will instead diffuse over various factions.

We've seen throughout history that the United States frequently addresses the problems of cyclical shifts by recourse to the tax code, considered the obvious solution to the problem of wealth distribution and prices. Yet the United States has developed massively and predictably. Looking at the chart below that tracks GDP growth from 1880 until 2010, the only significant decline was during the Great Depression, and, while noticeable, the more important fact is the consistent upward pattern of growth. The United States has maintained a steady and dramatic growth pattern in which all of the other cycles we have spoken of were merely minor dips and barely visible variations on a firm trend line. When we recall the great pyramid the United States was to construct, conceptually it looks like this.

There is no reason to believe this trend line will shift, and every reason it will continue. This in spite of the manic-depressive nature of the American soul. The fear that there is danger lurking behind the new prosperity will continue to haunt, reemerging as it has in recent years as a dominant theme. During the high points of the narrow cycles, there will be a belief that all dangers have been abolished, which is then shattered when minor events intervene.

Thus, the shift in economic policy will take place within the framework of normal economic development. But there is a deeper

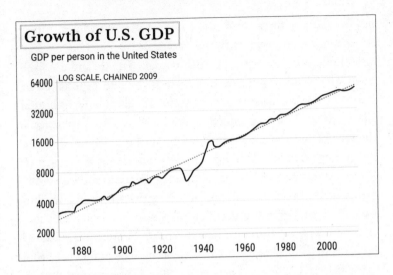

Growth of U.S. GDP

GDP per person in the United States

LOG SCALE, CHAINED 2009

social reality emerging that will define a new necessity for American society and will therefore be driving the new technology, social structure, and the very texture of the era.

The core problem of the next sociopolitical cycle will be demographic. I pointed this out in *The Next 100 Years* when I wrote that one of the central problems was the decline in birth rates and the extension of life expectancy. In 2018, the birth rate in the United States was the lowest ever. It has declined in all native-born ethnic groups.

Perhaps even more significant, life expectancy has expanded dramatically according to the national statistics office of the Census Bureau. This can be seen in life expectancy measured from birth, which has doubled in a century from about forty years to about eighty. But even more significant is life expectancy of people after age sixty-five. This eliminates the effect of infant mortality's decline on life expectancy. Fifty percent of all sixty-five-year-old males will live longer than age eighty-five, which is 9.2 percent higher than it was in 2000. Fifty percent of all women will live past eighty-six years. By comparison, in 1900, half of all men and women would not live past age forty-seven (these numbers are for whites; African Americans are consistently two years less).

So life expectancy is rising, birth rates are falling, and the likelihood of this continuing is extremely high. Life expectancy has increased due to medical advances and the decline of industrialism. Industrial mass production required continual presence in the factory and was physically draining, making maintaining one's health very difficult. With the decline of industrialism and the rise of service and technology industries, concentration on health maintenance became commonplace. Negative habits like smoking have declined, and more attention to exercise and diet has become common. This focus on health will expand. Simultaneously, developments in medical research are accelerating. The number of people living to over a hundred expanded by 44 percent between 2000 and 2014, according to the Centers for Disease Control.

The decline in childbirth is linked closely to the ability to control reproduction through birth control, urbanization, and declines in infant mortality. Urbanization was the key. In agricultural society, having many children who can become productive at an early age was important, as was the case in early industrialism. But in mature, urban societies, children are purely a cost center. With the extension of life expectancy, adolescence, defined as the period when someone can reproduce but cannot earn a living, has expanded dramatically. Unlimited reproduction now impoverishes a family, so fewer children satisfy the need to procreate.

But we must also note the early stages of the redefinition of the family. The first phase was the end of the notion that the bride must be a virgin at marriage. The second was the beginning of the idea that living together before marriage was acceptable. We are now in the midst of a redefinition of sexuality and of the family. The force that kept the heterosexual family in place and essential was the reality of agricultural and industrial life. The ability to have children demanded a male-female legal commitment and a marginalization of those outside the system. With the decline of the pressures of industrialism, and control and minimization of the number of children, the underlying gender realities emerge, and the institution of marriage becomes optional.

What is evolving is a collapse of traditional marriage and massive uncertainty regarding relationships. Some studies report a decline of sexual activity, decline of emotional commitment, and so on. What is created then is the anguish of freedom. When there is no rule as a guide, you confront the problem that it is not clear what to do. This represents a fundamental restructuring of deeply held rituals of life and the intense resistance of traditionalists to this process. This will be a part of the sixth cycle's politics but a declining part. Traditional marriage was an economic necessity, aligned with religious beliefs. With the end of the bond of economic necessity, the birth rate will obviously decline.

At the same time, this will be mitigated by the increase in life expectancy. Another 20 percent increase in life expectancy in the population as a whole will create a cohort that could for a time compensate for the loss of population. But for this to happen, life expectancy alone is not enough. There has to be a suppression of degenerative diseases that currently turn the older cohort into massive consumers of resources rather than producers. Diseases that kill quickly are economically sustainable. Keeping people alive who can't produce is economically debilitating.

Therefore, the need is for a massive revolution in biological research applied to medical care. And as we've seen in past cycles, it is the need that drives technological productivity. A range of diseases must be eliminated, such as Alzheimer's, Parkinson's, and others that render the elderly not only non-contributors but drains on society and the economy. But to do this, the underlying biological processes will need to be understood far better than they are now, and then a medical system able to apply the treatments' cost effectively must be in place.

One answer is a federal government that operates on the principles of decentralized and agile management described before. The government is the primary funder of medical research, and given the magnitude and importance, both social and personal, the demand for agile basic research follows. Second, a health-care system must be created that does not follow the current federal model of ultra-centralization and ultra-complexity but that can marshal the resources without paralyzing with fragmentation and micromanagement.

At all levels, there will be a loosening of bonds. The tight and stifling bonds of the federal government will be broken. The bond that tied the microchip to the vision of high tech will be broken. The alliance system that bound the United States to nations it had little interest in will be broken. America will be changing its direction as it always does when a new cycle begins. And so will the bonds that tied individuals together. Human beings are bound by traditions, and the traditions turn into rituals. The most important, the rituals of life such as birth, marriage, being a man, and being a woman, are fraying in the fifth cycle. The redefinition of sexuality is one force, changing the meaning of marriage. The attempt to redefine gender—what it means to be a woman and what it means to be a man—is under way. As the obligation of men and women to each other changes, so does the meaning of earning a living, saving for the future, and so on. The changing of particular obligations calls into question all obligations. This at first liberates and then leaves you alone, perhaps playing video games with adversaries you have never met.

The breakdown of rituals can't be permanent. The burden of living a life without any external expectation is liberating, but liberation also can leave someone at a loss for what to do next. A man once knew that it was his place to confront a heartless world in a struggle to make a living. A woman once knew that it was her place to create a haven for the man and children in a heartless world. That is still a choice, but a choice is not an obligation. Old obligations are collapsing, and the sixth cycle will create a new sense of what the order of life will be like. And all of this connects to the main issues of the cycle: the decline of the birth rate and the extension of life expectancy. Our rituals were built around an early death and the urgency to reproduce rapidly. Death is no longer imminent, and reproduction is an option. Therefore, the traditional family will be redefined. What are the obligations among people when life stretches to nearly a century and children are one option among many others?

This goes back to our early discussion of the invention of the United States. The founders sought to balance liberty and obligation. For them it was a political question. In the sixth cycle, it will be an existential one, defining who we are as individuals. The United States will face this more deeply than other countries, because American wealth creates many possibilities and those possibilities become endless.

Social media embodies this. It is a place of anonymity where you can reinvent yourself many times. It is a place where you can be heard but not known. And this is its mortal problem. In the end, for all of the distance the microchip has made possible, human beings must know whom they are speaking to. This is not a very profound truth, but it is the truth that the believers in social media have missed. But all media have their moment. The third cycle had radio. The fourth had television, and the fifth had the computer. At each step, human attention focused more on the delivery system than on other humans. Today, when you walk into a bar, there are no debates or seductions under way. Men and women sit looking at their phones.

But here there is an oddity. Television absorbed you. The cell phone connects you. Granted it is a strange and unprecedented way, as the rise of texting has superseded the prime purpose of the phone—a conversation hearing another person's voice. But as distorted as the connection might be, the phone, and its obsessive use, speak to the craving we have for other people. It is a caricature of human relationships, but a hunger for them as well. It doesn't create the loss of bonds. That was created by a shifting reality. The phone and even the text message are representations of the unwillingness of human beings to be simply alone. Social media is too anonymous to survive as a social foundation in the sixth cycle. But the human connection, frayed and chaotic, is still there.

If birth and death are at the center of the age, and the rituals for both are in tatters, the hunger for companionship is still there and asserting itself constantly. Since the invention of the telegraph, technology has been at the center of our communications. Therefore, the expectation is that the sixth cycle will have a new communication technology at its center. It won't. It won't, because communication technology has reached its reductio ad absurdum. It has become so thin in its efficiency that it cannot sustain the emotional needs of a human life. What will actually happen is the transcendence of the microchip culture and an aggressive reassertion of community, not perhaps with the old rituals, but with a culture that has at its center the avoidance of loneliness. The self-imposed loneliness of the microchip cannot sustain itself in human relations. It imposes rituals as all things human do. But they are rituals that may be addictive but can't be satisfying. In this, there will inevitably be a return to the past. Or more precisely, moving the computer into its limited place re-creates the past.

The hunger for AI represents the end point, because it proposes, at its most extreme, a replacement for human beings. Having the ability to think, it can replace human judgment in driving cars. But the claim is far-fetched. In order to create an artificial analogue of something real—such as intelligence—it is necessary to understand how we think. No one really understands how our minds work. The sterile logic of computers and their programs don't begin to grasp how we think. Thinking is far from a logical process. When I write, I suddenly discover things via a sense of excitement, and I don't know where it comes from. An analogue of intelligence is impossible until we come to understand thinking. In the meantime, we can have more powerful programs doing important things, but we will not have emotions, and without emotions there is no intelligence.

But AI takes an important place in all of this. The advocates of AI think that this would be a triumph of humanity. Apart from issues like jobs and computer failures, AI would undercut the necessity of humans for each other. We come together out of economic and other necessity. We remain bonded out of the pleasure in the fact that we are both human. AI, if it worked, would undermine the necessity that brings us together. The accidental insight and encounter are at the heart of human intelligence, and artificial intelligence, if it could be created, would destroy them by its inhuman efficiency.

Technological enthusiasts always extrapolate too far. When airlines began flying 707s, the dream was a rocket that would take us from New York to London in an hour. When electricity became commonplace, it was believed that all human mental function could be explained through electricity. Pictures from the 1930s of what cities would look like saw mile-high towers, highways in the sky, and no hint of a tree. Three things usually occur. First, moving technology beyond where finance and safety can take it. Second, using a technology you know and imagining that the whole world can be explained by it. Third, imagining a world that looks marvelous on paper but would be a nightmare in which to live. Some of course may come to be, and many others will press forward. But technology is a poor guide to what comes next. The reaction to technology is frequently not what the technologists want to see.

There is a revolt against the automobile today, especially in cities, that would have been inconceivable a generation ago. There is an abandonment of conventional television. Shortwave radio used to be a way to listen to the world. No one uses it any longer. The most solid technologies, things that were at the center of the way we do things, pass away with remarkable swiftness. When did you last receive a telegram? The computer and Internet and cell phone will be here for a century, as the car has been. But just as a car is merely a tool to get around rather than what it used to be, the definition of your identity, so too the microchip-based technologies will cease being a marvel and become a tool. And that will happen in the sixth cycle.

A social and then political movement will arise toward this end. Loneliness is one of the most powerful forces in the world. People get sick, and I know who will take care of me if I do. As those who are in their thirties and have no children and maybe no partner grow older, and face half a century more of their lives, they will have to answer that question, and the discovery that there is no answer will be terrifying. Living a long life without anyone needing you, no one really caring if you live or die, is liberation, but the terrible implications of liberation emerge with time.

It is not technology that will solve the problem of anomie, of being alone in a crowd. Rather, it will be the personal desperation that anomie brings. And just as the fifth cycle created a social movement that broke down a range of traditions, expectations, and rituals, so the sixth cycle, accepting the collapse of old rituals, will need to create new ones, based not on the urgency of reproduction before you die but on a more leisurely realization that having options ultimately culminates in making choices. There are dangers in growing old healthfully, as there were in dying too soon. The social upheaval of the sixth cycle will be about this.

Moving toward some sorts of ritualized relationships is needed to create an element of predictability in people's lives. All human societies have rituals, and many of those rituals concern obligations to family and larger groups. I know of no society in which family doesn't exist, and it carries with it obligations. It is unpredictable what sorts of families will emerge and what the obligations will be, but the purpose of the family aside from raising children, caring for the ill, and creating a division of labor is to satisfy a human hunger for companionship. New forms normally emerge out of war, when a society is ruined and a new order imposed. In this case, there will be many electives available, creating a flexibility in line with the spirit of the cycle. I suspect the order will include traditions from the more recent past.

It is in the nature of rituals to flow from traditions, and traditions to reach back to the past. It is also in the nature of those honoring traditions to want to universalize their principles and rituals, first through persuasion and then through law. In other words, the new rituals, to some extent mimicking the old, will seek a legal standing. Rituals can be religious but presented as secular. Rules on the number of spouses permitted, the rights of property in a divorce, and the treatment of children are secularized impositions of moral values. As new values arise toward the middle of the sixth cycle, they will take on a political form.

The struggle will be along two lines. First, there will be the issue of the tax code. The tax on higher incomes will surge at the beginning of the sixth cycle. But the problem will be that the new medical developments will require massive private investment. The federal government funds basic medical research, that research may be turned into new drugs or treatments, and the federal government does not traditionally take that role and certainly won't after its restructuring. Investment money will be available but tight, and the pressure will be for a new shift in the tax code.

The first generation of the sixth cycle, those we call millennials who will then be in their fifties, have an ideological aversion to lower taxes in order to facilitate private enrichment, at least those on the Left do. But these tax cuts would be to create capital investing in the treatments of diseases of an extended life. Self-interest will supersede ideology. Just as tax cuts drove the microchip economy, so they will, in the 2050s, drive the transformation of medical care.

The children of what are called millennials will be the ones who revolt against the previous generations' rootlessness. They will be the ones who find computers and the Internet old-fashioned and creating powerful family ties modern. And they will also be asking the state to enforce whatever values emerge and are shared. The temptation to legislate moral ends transcends all cycles. Their elders will be appalled by the younger generations' rejection of their attachment to microchips and horrified at a return to a degree of order and ritual in their lives. The older ones will be the remnant of the old technocracy that had been defeated in the 2020s, and the younger will be the ones who incorporate a range of formerly hostile groups to form their own party. Who will be Democrats and Republicans is unknown and unimportant. They will be the heirs of the coalition that defeated the technocrats, and have taken several decades to define themselves fully, and assert their claim to power. And as they settle into power, the forerunners of the seventh socioeconomic cycle will emerge.

There is one issue I have deliberately not touched on to this point, global warming and climate change. This is not because it is not important but because it has become a subject of simplistic name-calling (which I prefer not to get involved in) and a complexity that I can't unscramble.

First, it is clear that the climate is changing. It is generally believed that although the climate has changed in the past dramatically, it has not changed this dramatically. From what evidence there is presented by paleoclimatology (the study of prehistoric climates), this is the case, and I am not qualified to dispute it, so I accept it.

Second, it appears that this climate change is being driven by human activity. If the rate of change is as rapid as it appears, then I see no other force that can be driving it.

Third, I am unsure of what the world will look like at various levels of warming. The problem is that prediction depends on modeling (a subject I know a little about) and effective modeling of change depends on understanding all of the variables, their baseline interaction, and the impact of new forces on the variables. To know that, it is necessary to have a comprehensive understanding of how the climate works and to be able to model it. The level of understanding we have of how the climate works has expanded dramatically, but there remain many unknowns, particularly on isolating all the variables and measuring the impact of new variables being added to the atmosphere.

It is clearer that the climate is changing, and I am open to the claim that it is changing in a calamitous direction, but I am not certain. Many of the press releases are drawn from very limited studies relating a few variables. In isolation, they create a compelling argument for outcomes that would harm human beings. But given that there is no comprehensive model of the climate, it is possible that an unknown variable might moot the findings. The system as a whole might create outcomes different than the parts would indicate.

In addition, the idea that the outcome is negative is applied globally, but complex systems normally have complex effects. For example, we know that at one point in the past the Sahara was a rich and fertile garden. We know it is now a desert. Assume for the moment that rising oceans would inundate coastal cities but that the Sahara and other wastelands would bloom again. Would that trade-off be good or bad for humanity? In any event, there is no model that turns discussions of global climate into a more specific forecast.

I am always reminded of the population explosion that members of the Club of Rome, a prestigious group, said in 1970 would lead to global starvation by the year 2000. They were not alarmists. Looking at food production and at population growth rates globally, their forecast was accurate. It didn't turn out, because they didn't anticipate a dramatic increase in food supply because of Norman Borlaug's invention of miracle grains. Second, they didn't anticipate birth rates declining because of forces they never calculated. The universal belief in the population explosion was falsified by their failing to take into account something that had happened (miracle grains) and something that was in the very early stages of happening (declines in birth rate).

Those predicting population disaster were working from available data. The population was surging, and food production was static. The model they should have been looking at was too broad and complex to manage. I don't know if those speaking about climate change now are in error. I know that models, like that of the population bomb, tend to be faulty. So, I have not included it, because I don't know how to. It is my failure because while the climate is changing and humans are the likely driver of change, I have little guidance on how this might affect the American Southwest as opposed to the Northeast.

I have also neglected the subject because the probability of significant action is a political matter requiring global action, and I am confident that won't happen. The cost of restructuring lives to reduce greenhouse emissions will be staggering and must not be minimized. It will involve a significant decline in standard of living, including in places like China, where the standard of living in much of the country is always at a danger point.

The newly developing countries will not shift, because they cannot withstand the instability resulting from changes. In the advanced industrialized world, there are two political problems. First, no one is saying that disaster will occur next year. Most people measure their concerns by their distance in time. Climate change may not come, and if it comes, it will come after I am dead, so I'm not going to pay the price for an uncertain solution, or so the reasoning goes. The second reason is that the people who are most concerned about climate change are people who are least trusted. Climate change is seen as the most recent attempt by these people to seize control of the state and regulate behavior. Therefore, I am not forecasting a global response to climate change, because I don't think there will be one.

While I am here, let me give a boost to something I thought would play a major role in solving the problem. Climate change is happening, humans cause it, but no one wants to pay the price in fixing it. Green technologies cannot carry the burden of supporting an industrial-consumer society. My vision is linked to the rockets being tested in west Texas. One way to end pollution by power plants generating electricity is space-based solar power. There is an endless supply of sunlight in space and plenty of room for fast collectors. The collectors convert the sunlight into microwaves and beam them back to earth to massive transformers turning them into usable electricity. This would end the overuse of hydrocarbons and perhaps end the danger of climate change.

Space-based solar power was something I forecast in *The Next 100 Years* that I am beginning now to think may happen. So, let me throw this in as rare advocacy on my part. It would be far cheaper than slashing energy use in half, would not cause a revolution, and would use available technology. Regardless of models, this should be done.

Conclusion: The American Age

The year 2026 will be momentous for the United States. It will be 250 years since the signing of the Declaration of Independence, 250 years since the American settlers declared themselves a people and set themselves on a course that led to war, to improbable victory, and to the writing of a constitution that turned them from becoming a people to creating a regime. It all began on July 4 of that year, and the story is still unfolding, as I have shown, in a distinct and uniquely American way.

What is most extraordinary about this is what America has become. It has gone from a third world country to a behemoth astride the world. It produces nearly a quarter of all the wealth produced in the world each year. Its military forces operate, wisely or not, throughout the world. It has troops deployed in over 150 countries, most on minor training missions, some engaged in battle, but whatever the mission, and whatever the amount, that is a startling number.

The founders intended the United States to usher in a new age of the ages. But we all intend things that we don't think will happen. Did the founders, nearly 250 years ago, imagine the United States as it has now become? I see hints in Jefferson and Washington.

Franklin's sense of irony probably made the thought too far-fetched. John Adams and James Madison were likely more concerned with the immediate than with fanciful dreams. But still it happened. America became an empire, in spite of rising up against the British Empire. What these men intended, what they expected, might have been different things. But in this case what happened ought to have happened.

The foundation of the American empire is not the military nor even the economy. It is rock and roll, T-shirts that say "Santa Barbara," and New York Yankee baseball caps. It is going to a conference of people from twenty countries, with everyone speaking perfect English because it is the only language they have in common. It is above all the computer and programming languages that exist only in English. It is people resenting and even hating the United States yet hoping their children might attend an American university.

The foundation of any empire is not guns, something that Hitler and Stalin never grasped. It is money, and the envy that brings. But more important than money or guns is the technology that represents the future and the culture that speaks of being contemporary. All lasting empires are empires of the mind and soul, empires that cause others to crave to emulate them.

The United States was not founded to be an empire. Yet it is. "Empire" has been a term of approbation since the American Revolution. But there are two kinds of empires. One kind is strictly exploitative such as Hitler's attempt at creating an empire. The second type of empire benefits from the empire but also creates a system of symbiotic relations that all benefit from. That empire is held together not only by imperial force but by the benefits the colonials obtain. So, the Roman Empire conquered other nations, yet the desire to be part of the Roman system, while not universal, was common. The same can be said for the Persian Empire. The empire moves from being a conqueror to an overseer of economic growth, trade, and peace that would never have existed otherwise. It is also an instrument for cultural transfer and cultural evolution.

In being a nation that others will emulate, in trivial and greater ways, the United States is fulfilling the intent of the founders. Almost 250 years ago, they spoke of creating a new age. The age was built on the moral values of the regime and the things that flowed from it. The republican form of government is now almost universal, existing imperfectly at best, just as the United States fails to be totally faithful to its founders. But just as La Rochefoucauld said that "hypocrisy is a tribute vice pays to virtue," even amid the universal imperfection most of the world would claim to be a republic, ironically even those who have monarchs. The rights that the founders spoke of may be trampled on, but those who do the trampling usually lie about it. Baseball hats, computer languages, and carrier battle groups are symbols of a very imperfect triumph in fact and a great triumph in principle. The world looks very different because of things the founders thought and said.

The dilemma facing the United States is finding a basis for sustaining it in a radically new American era that began in 1992. This era will last for at least a century, even though the United States has not become comfortable with the reality of its power nor developed a strategy that will support it. The challenge facing the United States globally is to devise a sustainable policy of empire, in a nation where power, wealth, and innovation are being constantly increased through the cyclical process we have developed. On the one hand, the United States needs to become like other very powerful nations. On the other hand, it must not give up the creativity and energy that drive it internally.

American strategy prior to 1992 was to use military force to pursue its interest. Its greatest triumph was in World War II, when, in addition to defeating Germany and Japan, it gained domination of the Atlantic and Pacific Oceans, securing the United States from invasion, if not nuclear war. Since World War II, the United States has consistently used the same strategy it adopted before it became an empire. Except for Desert Storm, the United States has failed to win a war since World War II. Successful empires use as little military force as possible, depending on the regional tensions between nations to maintain their interests. Britain did not send hundreds of thousands of troops to control India. It used the balance of power in India.

The emergence of the American empire coincided with America's longest and in many ways least successful wars, those against the jihadists. After 9/11, the United States began operating in Afghanistan, supporting and buying native armies to confront al-Qaeda. But over time these were replaced by U.S. ground forces, and the war expanded to Iraq. What had been a rational war turned into both an unwinnable war and one that would drain and distort American domestic life. Imperial wars exhaust the homeland when fought against forces that are not organized as regular armies and therefore cannot be defeated by superior forces.

This points to the problem of the United States' immaturity. A mature national strategy minimizes conflict because an empire, with forces present in 150 countries of the world, has an endless possibility for conflict and war is more often initiated by its opponents. This can destroy a nation's dynamism. At the same time, the access to the world's resources, markets, and innovations creates a dynamic society. Empire can't be abandoned, nor can it be simply embraced. It must be managed with maturity.

Maturity is the foundation of empires, and the United States needs to achieve that stability. However, it is not the foundation of American domestic life. The cycles I have discussed are constantly returning to the beginning, and each cycle is a new invention of what America is. After both institutional and socioeconomic cycles mature, the problems swirl into a crisis, and the solution is found in starting over. There is an inherent tension between the necessary prudence of foreign policy and the orderly immaturity of the cycles.

The new cycles emerging in the 2030s will, as I've discussed, solve the problems of the current cycle and pose the problems for the new one. That will be 2080 for the socioeconomic cycle and around 2105 for the institutional. It's hard to really imagine the failure that will end each cycle. It would make sense that the socioeconomic cycle will fail because it will confront the pressures created by the radical change in the length of life given the new technologies we see coming. The elderly have wisdom, a sense of what human life is about, and what things are important and what are not. They don't always have the latest knowledge or use the latest technology. I used to be fascinated by computing. About a decade ago, I stopped caring. People younger than I am know far more than I do about computing. From my perspective, I have learned that computers are less important than love, that they may even interfere with the ability to love. Now, that may be either wisdom or crankiness, but it is not knowledge. As Americans live even longer with some regularity, the country may become wiser but less knowledgeable. And given that knowledge is essential to driving the cycles forward, the crisis of 2080 may well be built around the heavy weight of a large elderly population, in good health and filled with wisdom but unable to move beyond a cycle that's failing because of their presence and power.

As for the institutional cycle, the solution that will emerge in the federal government is one in which its internal functioning will shift, with the rigidity of regulation giving way to the use of increasing judgment among decision makers, from the public on up. In addition, there will be a resurrection of local political systems that have as their purpose representing individuals in dealing with the federal government and holding the federal government accountable for its performance. This will solve existing problems but not the problem that might well occur next. Our current institutional system has a minimum age for voting but not a maximum age. As life expectancy increases and the birth rate stabilizes at a low level, the population will be skewed to the elderly, whose interests will be very different from those of the younger voters. The elderly will become a larger voting bloc, based on longer life span, than they are currently. In addition, the dynamism necessary to the cyclical nature of the United States may seep out of the system. The elderly will be productive, but there is a part of creativity that is found in the young. It is possible, one could guess, that at a certain point the question will become putting a cap on the upper age for voting, or the vote over a certain age counts less than others. The extension of old age will have many consequences, and this may be the one on which the twenty-first century pivots.

The United States is becoming more mature by the nature of demographics. With that maturity comes wisdom, which is needed to maintain a foreign policy. But with that wisdom is the lack of energy needed to maintain the resilience of the United States that leads to the cycles. This tension was in a way at the heart of the founding. The founders were prudent in foreign policy. Their hearts might have been with the French Revolution, but their trade was with Britain, and the United States acted maturely in allying with England. At the same time, the cycles were constantly bringing the United States back to a kind of rebirth, and in each cycle we see a degree of imprudence needed to challenge the solid foundations of the mature cycle.

The founders were mature, prudent men. It was the nation that was immature and imprudent. It consisted of adventurers and risk takers, people who roamed where opportunity drew them and who lived the life they wished. For all the cycles we have gone through, it is not very different today. Many families have flung themselves apart with parents and children pursuing careers and opportunities hundreds or thousands of miles from each other. In the United States, it is possible to reinvent yourself, just as it is possible to relocate yourself. And it is possible to destroy yourself and others with you.

This is what makes the United States unique from other countries. All nations contain some elements of wildness. None have institutionalized the chaos as has the United States. It is this wildness that manifests itself in our cycles, mirroring the lives of individuals. They are born to overthrow reality; they create a new and unprecedented solution, much of it spreading around the world. The cycle drowns in its own successes and weaknesses in the seemingly reckless overthrow of all that was solid and found wanting. It is a country that has introduced revolution within the framework of the founding and institutionalized courage on all levels.

At the heart of this is the culture of technology. It is not unique to America, but it still is quintessentially American. In a book by Arthur Koestler on Stalin's purges, the protagonist, sitting in his cell, wonders what is happening in the world, having not read a newspaper in months. He wonders if the Americans have invented time travel. This gives you a sense of how the world, even in the 1930s, thought of America. No great art, no deep thought, no brilliant strategy, but a country capable of extraordinary feats of technological brilliance.

The new technology that will exist will be one that extends healthy life expectancy. In a world of declining population, this is the problem to be solved, and it will be solved by science. But as I have said, this will create a new problem. A nation dominated by the elderly, however vigorous and healthy, is a nation dominated by the old. It is dominated by the wisdom needed to manage an empire, but that same wisdom would paralyze the cycles that move America along. Youthful ignorance makes the impossible possible, by not knowing what is impossible and not making reckless things impossible but making them real. And in that recklessness is the future.

The fourth institutional cycle will be well suited to a healthy, aging population. It is about bringing common sense and wisdom into governance. They will threaten the socioeconomic cycles because age brings with it a sense of perspective. A sense of perspective, and what is needed is the reckless bravado of a Steve Jobs or a Henry Ford. So the problem that will emerge in the coming cycle will be that medicine will solve the problem of a declining size of the population and then create a socioeconomic crisis that will deeply divide the country.

Other countries will deal with this differently. The United States will deal with it as it always does, with its citizens going through a decade of intense political rage at each other, accompanied by an economic crisis and a social one: the old against the young, and the problem of innovation leading to instability. Finally, the political process will create a solution, with a failing president who worships the old cycle, followed by one who will claim credit for presiding over the new cycle and its solutions.

America is a country in which the storm is essential to clear the way for the calm. Because Americans, obsessed with the present and future, have difficulty remembering the past, they will all believe that there has never been a time as uncivil and tense as this one. They will wait for the collapse of all things and loathe all those who produced it—which will be those with whom they disagree. It will be a time of self-righteous self-certainty, hatred, sometimes murderous, for those they despise. And then the patterns of history work their way through, using the raw material available. American power in the world will sustain itself, because the power of a country like the United States, a vast economy and military and seductive culture, does not decline because it is hated. All empires are hated and envied. Power is not diminished by either.

The permanent things in America's founding—our rights and the Constitution—serve to drive both the prudence and the recklessness of the country. And it is the combination of these two things that has allowed the United States to evolve over nearly 250 years of stability and chaos. There is no evidence of it ending. The current storm is nothing more than what is normal for this time in America's history and our lives.

Acknowledgments

A book that took five years to write by its nature accumulates many debts. I can't thank enough those who spent their time trying to make this a better book. In particular, I want to acknowledge Marvin Olasky, Bill Serra, and David Judson, who didn't have to read this but were happy to do so and gave feedback in the early stages. Then my colleagues at Geopolitical Futures who had less choice but were nonetheless very helpful, including Antonia Colibasanu, Allison Fedirka, and especially Jacob Shapiro. Stacy Haren, the graphics designer from Geopolitical Futures, did a thorough and expert job on the graphics and maps.

Jim Hornfischer has been my agent through four previous books and shows no sign of giving up yet, so my thanks go to him for his handling of both me and the publisher. He always gives me useful feedback on the manuscript, even when I don't ask for it.

Most important, my editor at Random House, Jason Kaufman, has worked with me now on five books, and he deserves my utmost appreciation for his superb editing and for not throwing in the towel when we disagree over critical sections. His assistant editor, Carolyn Williams, also made this book much more readable, and to them both I'm truly indebted.

My gratitude to my children and grandchildren, whose forbearance while I spent holidays and vacations writing "the book" has finally paid off. Until the next one!

For my beloved Meredith, without whom no book of mine would ever begin or end.